FOR THE LOVE OF DREAM

Intro to Tending Your Nighttime Dreams

Marilyn O'Brien, PsyD

Cover image: *The Sorceress* by John William Waterhouse

ISBN 978-0-578-68045-3

This book is dedicated to my husband, Mark, whom I love to the stars and back. He is my greatest supporter and has always believed in me. He's taught me to rise above the small stuff, to have an inner strength that the outer world cannot dismantle, to carry the load and do the deeds I was meant to do in this life, to have challenges bring out the best in me and not be disheartened by them. Mark gives more than he takes, and I want him to know that I see that. May the person I am and I am becoming offer you back all that you deserve in life.

Contents

Acknowledgements

D r. Stephen Aizenstat, the founder of Pacifica Graduate Institute in Santa Barbara, is truly the life-changer and shape-shifter of my dream tending journey. My gratitude for this teacher, my mentor and friend, is immense for he has believed in me, listened to me, has offered a sense of equality, and has given me the greatest gift—that of the love of dream.

Along the way, he has provided fertile ground for me to grow, learn, and lead others in the training programs. Stephen Aizenstat envelops the dream world with his belief in nature and her ability to join us, or maybe more so, for us to join her in her depths where we can all connect and bring about change. One of his favorite quotes is, "You only have to let the soft animal of your body love what it loves..." by Mary Oliver. Stephen's love for dream stems from this place within him, and it is what he taps into when teaching us dream tending and working our dreams. As he works from this place, one feels his love for the dreamer, the dream, and images. As I work from this place, I, too, feel the presence of love.

Heidi Pace, my dear friend, who I love with all my heart, led me into the love of dream tending by guiding my first major dream 25 years ago. We met at Pacifica Graduate Institute and have worked dreams ever since 1992. Heidi has believed in me and has pushed me and poked me, along with other friends, to write this book, and to take it and myself out into the world.

Russell Lockhart is a Jungian analyst who has touched my soul with his writings, such as *Psyche Speaks; Dreams, Bones, and the Future*; and *Eggs are Words*, along with his personal communications of support as he egged me on to be daring and courageous in what I say and share. His belief and support that women are the carriers of the water and must step up to lead us to the next evolutionary stage, lit my torch. He encourages me to follow my urges, and I have been rewarded ten-fold in that it has allowed me to step out into the world and have a freedom of movement because something greater than myself is behind those urges. His question of "What is emerging?" as I tended my dreams still guides me to deepen my explorations. Thank you, Russ, from the bottom of my heart.

And as part of this presence of love in writing this book, I want to acknowledge the dream groups and dream tending friends who have walked this journey with me through the years. We have shared dream after dream with each other, slowly exposing our vulnerabilities with joy, tears, laughter and appreciation that resulted in such a greater depth of connection. These dreamers truly listened deeply into my dreams and were instrumental in me stepping onto my path. They saw in my dreams, first, what I did not—that a book was waiting in my future to be written. So, with my heart full of love for those who encouraged and pushed when needed, I begin.

And last but not least, my editors, Val and John Bowman, embraced this book with joy and enthusiasm. They merged the editing process quite effortlessly with the voices of my dreams that were asking to be heard in their own unique style. They dove in, heart and soul, believing in this book. Many synchronicities happened in the process of editing which affirmed our bond of friendship and importance of dreamwork.

Foreword

Have you ever wondered what comes awake when your eyes are closed? Dreams come, sometimes beautiful and exciting, other times nightmarish and threatening, yet always carrying something of a "gift" from what lives behind the veil. How can you unwrap this gift from the dream time? How can you find the value and discover the genius alive in the dream images that visited last night? In this beautifully written and artful book, Marilyn O'Brien offers you her ensouled guidance. Her expertise as a Dream Tender combines with her deeply felt desire to make this practice both easily accessible and personally rewarding.

Marilyn offers you a way of approaching dreams that invites their wisdom and intelligence to come forward and be known. She experiences dream Images as "alive," and, yes, "embodied." In these pages you will discover that tending dreams is like hosting a guest in your home. Marilyn tells of first preparing the reception, then taking the time to listen to who in particular arrives, then even offering, perhaps, a glass of wine and hors d'oeuvres. Only then do you meet the dream visitors in ways that help you listen deeply to the teaching stories they will tell.

There is a saying in Dream Tending, "a dream loves to be met in the way of a dream," rather, than at first, in the ways of interpretation or analysis. Marilyn O'Brien is a master at meeting dreams on their own ground, in the landscape of imagination, art, and story. Think about it, when you arrive at someone's home, how disappointing and off-putting it is to be met by a hundred questions and told what should happen next! Marilyn expertly offers artistic skills, storytelling tools, and approaches of enactment that allow you to hear the wisdom stories and life teachings that arrive with each dream. Her approach animates the "living images" in dreams with care and special regard.

In the pages that follow, Marilyn invites your curiosity into one of life's greatest resources, the healing powers of dreams. She offers the way to a dream-centered life, one filled with wonder and creativity. Here you will embody the soul-centered beauty of the living psyche, the birthplace of dreams. Of the many articles and books written about Dream Tending, I find *For the Love of Dream* to be uniquely tender, beautifully written, and heartfelt. A must read for all students of the Dream Tending approach and an extraordinary introduction for those with a desire to explore the mysteries and teachings of dreams.

—Stephen Aizenstat

Introduction

A ren't dreams a curious thing? They can be so bizarre, scary, funny, nonsensical, and sometimes it seems like there is no way they could be important. Yet, something haunts us, makes us wonder, makes us ponder, "Where do these dreams come from?" and "What can they mean?" I believe that these questions are about a desire to discover more of the mystery that lies behind our everyday life. Somewhere within, us we know there is more, and then we have these curious dreams—it might be a dream with a woman's voice saying loud and clearly, "You listen outside; now listen inside." Or it might be a dream where you are driving a car and the brakes won't work, and you wake up with your heart pounding! There are dreams where you are in a pool of water and an exotic man swims toward you and kisses you. You wake up with a delicious smile on your face, but then wonder if you should feel guilty because your husband is sleeping next to you. This is all such rich and amazing dream material that your soul is offering up to you for exploration and integration.

My training in Counseling Psychology with a specialization in depth psychology, and in particular the teachings of Dr. Aizenstat on Dream Tending, offer a style of dream work that opens an inner world of images that are wanting to be in relationship with us and to our outer world. Going back to the question most of us ask, "What does this dream mean?" I have to confess I ask the same thing. It is so automatic. We want the answer right now, and we assume that there is a direct answer—we just do not know the code to unlock it.

Dreams come to us via the right brain, which is the part of the brain that connects with the unconscious—it speaks in images, metaphors, feelings, and symbols. Dream images freeze or scamper away if the left, logical brain immediately begins to scrutinize and try to explain what they mean in a linear manner. If the dream wanted to be worked in that way it would have been delivered in that manner, and then we would have analyzed it, boxed it up, and set it aside. Instead, we are invited into an imaginal dreamscape with child-like play and wonder, as we begin developing our senses as trackers in the woods following the crumbs or tracks of the dream images. Once upon a time as a child we knew how to follow in this way of exploration and play so let's rediscover this again together.

And so, with child-like awe, I will share a dream story. *I see this lush, freshly mowed grass and walk over to this almost mossy section of it. Leaning down, I grab it and lift up this clump of sod. Underneath is a beautiful, sparkling pendant. I am shocked. The stones are yellow with an amber center.* I had such a visual sense of this pendant, the shape, the color of the stone, and so I drew it in my dream journal. I wondered and pondered why this was in my dream. I explored the landscape, and what the colors represented, and how I felt so amazed by this discovery.

A month later, my husband (not knowing anything about this dream or image) presented me with a birthday gift. I again was shocked as I opened the case to find this same pendant that was in my dream; it was now being given to me by my husband! Well, the dream story does not end there. I loved this pendant so much and because we were going on a three-week trip, I very carefully hid it. Yes, you guessed it. I couldn't remember where I hid it. I frantically searched the house over and over again looking for this necklace pendant. I truly felt that the dream had given me some kind of hint of where or how to find the dream, but I couldn't figure out the clues. All I knew was there was this soft moss and earth, and this motion of lifting or pulling up.

So, days passed. I even did a prayer to Ganesh, the finder of lost items, and kept hoping, but I was getting more and more discouraged. And then one day, I opened a drawer in my closet, and again opened this black velvet square earring case. Empty. But then somehow my fingers reached in and with the same motion of lifting the moss clump, I lifted up the velvet piece that holds the earrings, and hidden underneath was the pendant! I truly believe that movement of lifting the clump of grass from the dream led me to lift the velvet to discover the pendant. Such a mystery it had been of first receiving the pendant I had already dreamed about and then to have the same dream hold a clue for finding it. And *that* is what makes me love dream work. I had tended and valued that dream by writing it down and taking note of the details and consciously carried this dream with me.

Staying in the Moment

A major goal of this book is to have you feel confident and comfortable in your ability to use dreams as a map to guide you on your soul's path. I have found there to be a love and joy of the divine that opens as I take these steps, and She, too, is stepping toward me. My hope is to break down the steps of the dream tending process for everyone, especially beginners, to comfortably begin exploring their dreams. (I will be referring to the dream tender and the dreamer as "she" just for the ease of writing—truly it can be either a "she" or a "he.") As we go forth, we will discover there are multiple ways of tending our dreams. You can examine your dreams Individually, with a Partner, or, to deepen the experience further, share this exploration in a Group. The steps and skills provided may be used interchangeably within all the situations.

Before we do this, we will look at the different ways that dreams enrich our lives from predicting the future, to giving guidance and messages—leading us into wholeness. I will give advice and ideas on how to remember and record your dreams. We will delve into how to enter the dreamscape of our dreams and learn ways to help the dream open up to begin revealing its messages. I will offer tools and guidance to help you with the dreadful visitations of nightmares. There is a chapter on how to deepen your dream work using art, writing, and movement. At the end of the book there will be Summary Sheets, which can be used as reminders of the steps in approaching this work.

In the process of working with dreams, you are more than likely to find that there is quite a mystery happening right before your eyes as synchronicities occur, such as your dream images showing up in your outer world or dreams guiding you in choosing jobs or helping in relationships. Because nature is present in this work, there's a good chance of finding an aliveness that might have previously been missing in your life. And for sure there is a belief and trusting that something greater than us, something I call the Other, has its hand in the mix as we work together to create an inner and outer world worthy and full of possibilities. Please, come join me in this exploration as we step through the portal and into the mystery.

Chapter 1:
WHY I TEND MY DREAMS

Dream work is soul work for me. It is a spiritual journey with guidance from my dream psyche that offers me the gift of dreams. What I began to realize is that there is a third element, a presence of *Other*, which enters the story. This presence changes the ordinary to the numinous when I tend my dreams with an open heart and open mind—these images and stories begin to take on a life of their own. Who or what this Other is will be for you to discover. For me, there is a sense of God, my Higher Self, and a wisdom and mystery that is evolving as I evolve. I can do ordinary things in life and can do them pretty well, but when I leave room for and invite in the Other, then incredible insights and miracles occur and doors open that had not previously existed.

Because it is part of a secret or invisible world that we tap into in this work, I almost want to say it in a whisper. *These dream figures and images are Real.* There is a world behind our world that is ever present and existing at the same time as this one, and we have access to it as we lean into the dreamtime and what it has to offer. Stephen Aizenstat says, "We know... When our eyes close, when we dream, something else comes awake. From this point of view we know we have access to something bigger than ourselves." We are not the only ones dreaming—the world is dreaming and has a dream of which we can be a part.

Each time we work with a dream it is like creating a piece of art in which we are then invited to step into. But I want to be clear, this is not about learning to be an artist in the usual sense. It is about being open and available to a process that wants to come through you with a dream script or a story that's never been told. Some characters and places might be familiar, but the story always has a twist, familiar or not, that is be-fuddling, unknown, or bizarre. The next day you tell your friend, "I had this dream last night where I won an Academy Award, but I didn't even know what movie I had starred in!" And we wonder, "Why did I have *that* dream?" What a curious thing. My hope is for you to have some tools for exploring and discovering why these dreams come visiting and what messages they bring, so that you will become an adept dream tender.

With this idea of creating a piece of dream art, imagine taking a thir-ty-piece puzzle box with no picture on the cover, and now dump the piec-es onto the table and begin to explore how they might fit together. See the indiscernible picture pieces, and sense with your hands the shapes and edges of these pieces. What is it you already know of puzzle pieces? Can your fingers find the straight edges that are usually the outer edges of the puzzle? Are some of the pieces already connected, which helps make it a bit easier. By beginning in this way, without the full picture from the box cover, you are working totally opposite from what the linear left-brain would like you to be doing. It can be frustrating not knowing the picture at first. What is different when working a dream versus a puzzle is that these "pieces" have been delivered up by your own dream psyche.

As we explore the different pieces or parts of the dream, we will use little logical-mind effort, especially at first. It is so very important to ap-proach this dream work with a stance of Not Knowing. This came easily for me and gave me hope that maybe I actually could do dream tending. For others, this might be a challenge because it's necessary to "back burn-er" the left-brain, analytical thought process that thinks it does know.

Each dream piece has memories attached, the future attached, dream psyche humor attached and more. We just need to have curiosity and pa-tience. We are participating in being with a story picture that has nev-er existed before this moment—we mainly have our senses to guide us. Whether it is the dream-story puzzle developing or a dream script being acted out on an imaginary stage, you are the co-director and also the one playing all the different parts. Those of you who are hesitant or skepti-cal of being able to do this will just have to trust that child-like part of yourself that knows how to explore the inner and outer world with Curi-osity leading the way. Working with dreams challenges us to slow down and allow for this creative process, and with practice you will find your own unique style of doing this work. My love of Nancy Drew as a young girl fuels the fire of curiosity for what is hidden but present, along with my love of mystery. Who or what is hidden? Who or what is overseeing this piece of art unfolding? Oh, my! There is so much to discover! Dreams have many different treasures to offer.

The Future in our Dreams

> *You must give birth to your images. They are the future wait-*
> *ing to be born. Fear not the strangeness you feel. The future*
> *must enter you long before it happens. Just wait for the birth*
> *for the hour of the new clarity.*
>
> *– Rilke*

To believe that most of our dreams carry an element of the future is one thing, but to actually experience this can be amazing. I've had dreams of giving a particular presentation even before I knew I was ever going to give that particular talk. Dreams of me being pregnant or having a baby have been written in my journal and then new ideas or plans (like births) occur a few months later. Many times, it's only in glancing back through my journal that I realize that Dream Psyche had already forecasted the new idea and had been preparing me for it. Sometimes these images of the future have profound meaning, and sometimes they capture my atten-tion, and I might never know why.

While in New Hampshire with a friend who was looking at schools for her children, I had a dream. *This guy is driving around this large park-ing lot in this very peculiar Volkswagen bus with all these scientific gadgets on it and in it. End.* In real life, my friend visits this school the following day, and there in the parking lot is a VW bus with all these gadgets and antennas attached to it. The kids had taken this VW bus and made it a science fair project, and their teacher was the driver. This was straight out of my dream!

Now one might be tempted to ask, "What does this mean!?!" I will be honest with you and say I still don't know why this dream came. For whatever reason, Dream Psyche decided to show me a snippet of the fu-ture. One thing this occurrence did was to get my attention, and it punc-tuated a situation that could not have been coincidental. I reflected on the explanation that life is like a book that has already been written—it just depends on which page happens to open up. What if... what if that is really true and real? So maybe I got a sneak preview of the next day before it actually happened. Now it has a bit of a Nancy Drew mystery to it, and Dream Psyche is so clever. Once I realized that things that occur in dreams can actually end up in the outer world, I began to start looking at the outer world with different eyes and different ears.

Another night, Blue Tarp showed up in my dream and then the next day, I spotted at least fifteen blue tarps throughout the day. Of course, I asked the question, "Why blue tarps?" That particular color of blue shows up in my dreams and in my art constantly. I explored how tarps protect and contain, and many dreams since that time have more to say and more depth to them, but then I catch myself—what is simple and lights me up with an inward grin? Blue Tarp.

Through the Eyes of Aizenstat

> *Dreams are Alive*
> *Everything in the world is alive*
> *Dreams have a life of their own*
> *Everything is dreaming*
> *—Stephen Aizenstat*

Dream images not only live within us, but they exist all around us, in every animal, plant, and object of this world. I would hear Dr. Aizenstat say this, but to get it and embrace this did not happen overnight. But then things began to happen. I stepped outside one day and a breeze was brushing against my face in a way I had never experienced before. It felt like I was being kissed by the wind. This tingling, tender sensation was absolutely loving and so alive, and I began to wonder, "Is this what he means when he says, "Everything in the world is alive?" This discovery continued to unfold through the years in the outer world of nature as She and I began to know and have this different relationship and acknowledgment of each other. The voice of reason and logic had been keeping my world dry and flat, and by allowing imagination and dream to have a place in my life, it brought such life-changing richness to every experience.

Nature and Dream came together in a dream of mine called Soaring Violin. The setting is in the country.

I am visiting with a friend. I notice and hear something going on behind me. I turn and look, and someone is tossing a large violin through the air. It catches my attention as it is sailing and soaring through the air, flying higher and farther than I could ever imagine. And then it happens. The wind hits the strings and a beautiful sound is made. Oh my! I can't believe it! The violin is playing exquisite music as it sails through the air.

Soaring Violin is a dream that I explored using the techniques in the following chapters. By exploring and being with this dream in multiple ways, I was able to experience within myself the sensation of the soaring violin. I know deep in my soul the feeling and the music that is made when there is this visitation by the spirit of wind. To this day, when I reflect on the sensations of this dream, awe and excitement still visit as my body feels into the soaring violin that made such beautiful music. Now, can you begin to imagine into the sense of the world dreaming this dream?

Synchronicity

As you begin to be in the "flow" of life and working with the dream material delivered by your psyche, you will begin to see and experience synchronicities in your life. These are coincidental occurrences that happen with the sense of divine timing connected to a message. Synchronicities are affirming that we are on the right path, and they urge us on to the next step. Though we might be skeptical at first, something inside of us knows a message just came from the universe, punctuating the experience. It encourages us to continue looking in our outer world for signs that resonate in our inner world. For example, you might be extremely unhappy in your work but unsure whether to make a change. As you dwell on this one morning while hiking, you might see the following sign alongside the road: Dead End Job—This Way Out. The answer shows up right in front of you—*that* is synchronicity at work. Synchronicities occur a great deal more than we realize, but we must be conscious and paying attention for our

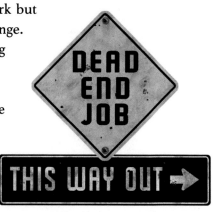

inner and outer messages and images to link up.

Recovery of a Memory or Experience

Unless we write our dreams down, they usually disappear as we get on with our day. For most of us, it is a particular dream that never disappears and can haunt us that lures us into asking more questions or seeking answers from professionals. Many of us have a scary childhood dream that lurks, while others might have a haunting, unforgettable dream as an adult. When I was 40 years old, I had the following dream that grabbed my attention and opened up the world of dream tending for me.

> *I am in a house when I hear a plane overhead. I know it is having problems and is going down. The plane turns into a helicopter—I can hear it. I call for help and gather things needed and rush out to the crash site. Upon arrival, there are three people: a pilot, a woman in my class who is angelic-like, and a man in my class who is a medical doctor. They are awake, then dead, then awake. I look over on a snowy hill and here comes a man to help. He's wearing a ski mask.*

It was during the tending of this dream with my friend that I uncovered the power of working with dreams because the tending uncovered me. As this dream came alive, and I looked closely at the helping man with the ski mask, it became a surgery mask. I slid right back into a childhood tonsillectomy surgery and found myself on the surgery table reliving the fear of the doctor coming towards me with a mask on. There was definitely a trauma that occurred for me during that surgery, either real or perceived. Other dreams have led me to believe it was more than just the fear of the doctor that caused such a trauma for me. It could be that I left my body or actually died momentarily during the procedure. The hospital lost my records so I will never know for sure, but what I do know is that so many things in my life began to make sense—why I shook so much when lights and focus were on me, why my throat would swell when I sang, why I held my breath to the point of sometimes passing out (entertaining childhood classmates). Yes, I was truly uncovered and began the journey back that was guided by my dreams.

Touchstone or Guiding Light Dreams

Dreams have given me more than just the unveiling of traumatic events or the offering of fascinating moments, such as I had with VW Bus and Blue Tarp from earlier. There are guiding dreams that advise and teach. These are important dreams because they have held so much value in their wisdom, not just for me but for many with whom I have shared the dreams. One is a dream from 20 years ago called Split by the Light.

> *There is an old cabinet with many drawers full of old pictures that I discover in the damp basement. I am concerned about the cabinet getting mildewed. We quickly begin to move this beautiful old piece of furniture up these stairs, but it begins to dry out too quickly, and it starts splitting. "Oh no! I've got to get it back to the basement quickly—I'm bringing it up too fast!*

This dream has been with me for years. What a beautiful way for Dream Psyche to tell me that I am bringing something up out of the unconscious too quickly or shedding too much light on a dream too soon. This dream also reminds me not to go directly to asking, "What does this dream mean?" We need to get to know the images in their landscape–here in the basement–before they are hit with the dryness and light of our everyday world.

Dreams and the Body

The dream of the recovered surgery trauma helped me realize just how involved the body is in this work. I became aware of the trauma that had embedded in and debilitated my body. I soon began to meet with a therapist who helped me give voice to these body symptoms. I also began having massages to release the emotional trauma. Marion Woodman, Jungian analyst and mythopoetic author, was one of the first Jungians to truly explore dream work along with honoring the body. She emphasizes that we must keep our awareness in the body:

> *Body work is soul work,*
> *Imagination is the bridge*
> *between body and soul.*
> *To have healing power,*
> *an image needs to be taken*
> *into our body on our breath,*
> *Only then can the image connect*
> *with the life force.*
> *Only then can things change.*
>
> *(Coming Home to Myself)*

Breathing, exercising, and doing our inner work helps us to develop and strengthen our body as a vessel so it may become the container and the conduit to amplify and transform the magnificent energy available to us. This energy that enters when our feminine and masculine energies are working together, helps us to "hold the tension" of adversity and difficulties along with the highs of awe and joy. Holding the tension can have such a feeling of discomfort, yet if we can stay with it, we are training and teaching our body how to not run away or bolt from conflict or scariness unless we truly are in danger.

Chapter 2:
REMEMBERING AND TENDING YOUR DREAMS

Remembering Your Dreams

How do we begin the process of remembering and working with our dreams? Most of us do not remember our dreams after a few hours of the morning has passed. Unless it was an absolutely terrifying dream, the dream seems to have a way of slipping back into the unconscious. It feels like something sliding right out of our hand and down the rabbit hole—it can be so disappointing. Some dreams are not ready to be looked at in the light of day and need to return to the oven for more cooking, but most dreams are asking to be noticed, and so how do we do this? First, begin by having that inner conversation with Dream Psyche and speaking of your commitment of wanting to remember your dreams. This is how I do it: "Dream Psyche, I would like to begin remembering my dreams—say this repeatedly. I need your help; I will do my part by writing my dreams in my journal."

The next morning or whenever the dream arrives, I remain in bed and in the same body position I was upon waking, and then I consciously rerun the dream in my mind by going over every detail I can recall. Many times, I start at the end of the dream, right where I was when I woke up, and then I head backwards toward the beginning. It's amazing what reveals itself. At first it might seem like there is hardly any recall, but then as you reflect, more of the dream begins to show up. It's important to note things such as time of day of the dream (dusk, dark, day, etc.) and the landscape. Is it my childhood home or a park that's unfamiliar? The more description you can give to the scene and the characters, the easier and more helpful it will be later as you write the dream down and then begin to work with it. Notice what feelings and emotions are present in the dream; for example, "I am upset at my husband for ignoring me. I cry, and I'm angry." A dream sometimes feels so vague that I can hardly capture it on paper, but I do the best I can. I suggest you go ahead and write, even if it feels like you are making it up, it is all good since the dream and the imagination come from the same source. If you are hesitant, then put parentheses around the part that feels "made up."

Not Remembering your Dreams?

Sometimes it takes awhile to begin to access our dreams. Everyone dreams, but the challenge can be getting these dreams to be remembered as we wake up. Here are a couple more suggestions to help with remembering dreams. Take a dream or dreams from your past, whether it was last year or as a child, and write them. Dreams never quit "giving" so go ahead and use these older dreams to practice dream tending until recall begins again. Keep in mind that Dream Psyche might not deliver another dream if there is a lingering dream that needs tending.

Secondly, begin to write down stories from your waking life. In using this material and writing it in story form, you are accessing the right brain that is the creative, imaginative part from which the unconscious flows. Writing stories that you've created in your imagination works, also. The point is that by writing and carving out time in your morning, you are truly sending the message to Dream Psyche of your interest in the imagination and dreamtime. Also, there is a total connection between enhancing the creative mind and the dreaming mind because both are sourced by the unconscious where Dream Psyche and Soul reside.

Thirdly, stress and drugs impact dream recall. If you are having difficulty recalling your dreams, know that the following items can impact recall and even the quality of dreams. It is vitally important to be getting a good night's sleep and the more consistent the better. The use of drugs including alcohol, mind-altering drugs, cold medicines, antihistamines, sleeping pills, and stimulants can substantially reduce dream recall in some people. Vitamin B deficiency has also been known to impact dream recall.

Recording your Dreams

Some people keep their journal right next to their bed so they can immediately write their dreams down. This is a great idea especially in the beginning and/or if you are waking in the middle of the night with a dream. I don't usually wake-up in the middle of the night, plus I don't want to disturb my husband, so my routine is to get up and go downstairs, fix a cup of tea, and then sit in my morning chair to write my dream. This works for me because I spent the time in bed reflecting on my dream prior to getting up. As I write my dream down, I write in present tense for it to be present in the here-and-now. For example, I might write "I crawl in the boat from the dock. I am excited about heading up the river. Wait! Whale swims towards me." Notice that I didn't say "the whale;" I said "Whale" as a proper noun. This is important for when we begin to animate the dream figures. Also notice things such as smells, voices speaking very distinctly, peculiar objects or people.

I use a spiral-bound, college-space notebook as my dream journal. I write the dream as clearly as I can because, many times, I photograph it to be able to share it with a friend or a dream partner. Some people have beautiful journals with a dreamy cover, others have a journal with no lines so they can also draw their dream. Some people type their dreams; others have found it helpful to record their dreams with a tape recorder or phone and then later write it down. It is truly a matter of style and what fits for you. I jot down at the top of the page what has been happening in my life the last couple of days. It's always a bit of a challenge to make the shift of taking the dream story/movie in my mind and getting it transferred into words on the paper. I add a title to the dream after I finish writing my dream. I try to not over think this but just write down what feels like the main focus of the dream. This title can also help me later to find dreams in my journal. Within the dream, if there is something with movement, directions, or placements, I have found it helpful to do a sketch that shows it. For example, if multiple people are sitting at a table in the dream, I will sketch it, and show where each person is sitting. After writing the dream down, I go ahead and write thoughts and feelings that are triggered by the dream. If the dream captures an event from the previous day I jot down a few notes or write about it. We are learning to be writers of stories by doing this process. Writing down what the inner eyes and inner ears see, hear, feel and experience takes trust of believing in the process and trust that it might be of some value.

At the bottom of the page I write down the feeling words in the dream. I begin to write down the associations that come up. Usually there's only one or two right off the bat. Every dream is different but, for example, I might realize that the number five (five boys, five circles) is a pattern showing up in multiple dreams. I might or might not recognize characters in the dream and will begin asking the question of "Why are they showing up today?" The other thing I will immediately take note of is "Where is the dream taking place?" I will jot down a few notes. At this point I feel awake but know I am in both worlds—the world of the dream and in my waking life but not fully awake and engaged in the day. I know this because one early morning my sister called needing my zip code at the same time I was writing down a dream that was located in Coloma, CA, where I used to live. I didn't realize until later that I gave her the zip code for Coloma, instead of my present day zip code. I was amazed when I discovered this, and it was so telling of how deeply I still was in dreamtime when she called.

Do I Work Every Dream?

Even with such a love for doing dream work, I would say at least half of my dreams are never tended—it just depends on my time availability and how the particular dream has grabbed me. I do write down all the dreams I am able to recall and a few notes with them, but many sit on the sidelines and get read here and there or I refer back to them as events in the future unfold. I confess, it's either the dreams that capture my attention and have great feeling in them, or ones that seem like a world dream that call to me to tend to them. Another thing that happens, and is why a dream partner is very helpful, I will be talking to a friend and will share a dream that feels like what I call a "nothing burger" and suddenly, with a little help from them, that dream can begin to open and surprise me with new awareness. Also, keep in mind that dreams aren't just worked once if the door to enter them has now been opened. They can stay present with you for days, months, and years depending on the dream. New layers can show themselves as dreams are re-visited, so what might have started as a dream I tended by myself, might later get tended by others resulting in new facets being revealed. It just depends on the dream and what it has activated within me and even with others.

I want to make the point here of just doing the best you can in remembering and writing dreams down and tending your dreams. If you truly are only able to write dreams down on weekends then do just that, otherwise you might do nothing at all and that would be sad. We all do what we can do including dream work. What I found for myself is that once I was hooked into the richness of this work, I began to make more time in my schedule—funny how those things work, time-wise.

Tending Your Own Dreams

If you are new to exploring your dreams, you will probably begin by working with your own dreams—which means you will be asking yourself questions of curiosity. Continuing from the work you did after writing the dream down in the morning, for example, what were the emotions in the dream, what is the landscape of the dream, what does this dream make me think of. You will explore definitions of words (even the ones you think you know) that can reveal hidden meanings; pulling a mythology book off the shelf because you are reminded of the story of Persephone; going to a dream book that mentions smoke because your dream had smoke in the distance; or googling on the computer—all of these things are part of the beginning of dream exploration whether you tend the dream yourself or work with others.

I have also learned to pay attention in my outer world during the day, of my dream themes or images showing up in the outer world—finding these synchronicities validates that I am on the right trail, and I make sure I get this recorded in my journal. Synchronicities are easy to forget.

Working Dreams with Others

My hope for you is that I can help you find a starting place for tending your own dreams, and then if you are interested in expanding this work, that you might eventually discover a friend or group to tend your dreams with.

This process is so very much about relationship, whether it is relationship with different parts of yourself as the dream images interact with each other or the relationship with others as a dream is told and then heard by another—something greater begins to open. I have several friends with whom I share dreams individually. It is amazing what Aha's you can have together with laughter, tears, and insights. I had a dream in which my friend Heidi, who is a lumberjack in the dream, gives me an old rusted bike to use to get to the next town. The tires are flat, and the chain is hanging off. In waking time, we are seriously looking and being with the dream when suddenly we both start to giggle and I say, "Thanks a lot, Heidi! What a friend you are! You are giving me a broken down and rusted up, useless bicycle!" And she says back, "Oh, I've got more where that came from!" There was truly high play from both of us. We belly laughed so hard we had tears rolling down our faces. We eventually gained more from the dream, but there was definitely the sense that Dream Psyche delighted in this playful meeting of two friends with the dream images.

By the way, it wasn't long after that, that old rusted bikes were found in the woods of Heidi's childhood ranch house where she and her sister helped her dad with his summer camp for kids. The synchronicities continued when her husband discovered a newspaper article that told of the previous owner who built the house in 1910. The article featured a picture of the man at age 80 holding the Old Rusted Bike he had ridden over 250 miles, years ago, to see his girlfriend whom he eventually married. What a rich sharing and amazing laughter came from the dream image of Rusted Bike.

Summary: Remembering and Tending Your Dreams

- **Have journal and pen ready** either next to bed or by your writing chair.
- **If you have difficulty remembering dreams say,** "Dream Psyche, I would like to begin remembering my dreams. Repeat this several times. I need your help, and I will do my part in writing my dreams in my journal."
- **When you wake up with your dream, try to stay in the same body position** in bed to recall the dream, remembering as much as possible. Do a review before rising.
- **Write date of dream. Write dream in present tense,** i.e., "Whale is swimming in River." Use Whale and not just "a whale." You are Naming it.

- **Give as much description as possible.** Time of day; era; landscape; characters.
- **Make a note or two of what has happened** in the last couple of days.
- **To jump-start dream work, write down previous dreams** and work with them.
- **If still not remembering dreams,** write in journal daily. Write down thoughts, feelings, and desires. Use your imagination, and write stories from your waking life.
- **Dreams can be affected** by stress, drugs (including alcohol), and Vitamin B deficiency.
- **Dream partners and dream groups** are extremely beneficial.

Chapter 3:
TELLING, LISTENING, AND EXPLORING THE DREAM

If I could give you four gifts right now, they would be an attitude of Deep Listening, Not Knowing, Curiosity, and Patience. Embedded within and all around each one of these is the presence of Love. When I am with a dream in this way, there is always an entry into the dreamscape in one form or another. Deep listening is a way of listening that uses all our senses in the body. You would think the Not Knowing would be easy for a beginning dream tender, but as we tend the dream, there is usually a bit of a panic within and a voice saying, "I don't know what this dream means! Nor do I know what to say next!" We might feel inadequate or unqualified. These feelings still visit me after I write down my own dream or after I hear someone tell their dream to me. Experience has taught me to stay calm, patient, and trusting of this mysterious process.

A Not Knowing attitude is the perfect place to start this work, for we never go after a dream directly. Dream images are like skittish animals, and so we must approach them gently, caringly, and respectfully. We sit with the dream, calming our own thoughts and body posture so we may be open to what presents itself from our dream guest. I use the terms Dreamer and Dream Tender to clarify the process. If you are working your own dream, then you are both the Dreamer and the Dream Tender, playing both roles by answering the questions yourself.

Many times, it is a nightmare that motivates people to begin looking at their dreams. Chapter 7 gives specific recommendations for working with nightmares. Nightmares can be terrifying and haunting, and they can leave us pretty shook up or unsettled. It can be helpful to know that Dream Psyche delivers nightmares to get our attention and to make the point that there is something very important for us to look at in our dreams and our lives.

Dream Tending Preparation

Before a dream is invited to be shared:

Relaxing and Grounding. Take 3-5 deep breaths. Relax. Feel the chair you are sitting in holding you. Imagine a cord or root going down from your tailbone and anchoring into the earth. Now visualize traveling up the cord through the body and out the top of the head and climbing into the heavens. Imagine it returning to the heart and connecting the two of you.

Calling in Guides. Know that you are not alone as the dream visits. Call in your guides, angels or ancestors. Feel the presence of love and respect. It might be a felt sense of a guiding presence or ancestor, such as your grandpa, that shows up. It could be God, Mary or those figures that carry his or her presence. Request that these guides be those that serve your highest purpose. If you feel unsure of their presence, still do the Calling and then don't worry, because over time, if not immediately, you will begin to sense you are not alone. Now, carry on.

Telling and Listening to the Dream Present Itself

When you are tending another person's dreams, ask them, "What dream has visited you?" Encourage your dreamer to take her time in telling the dream, and as the dream tender, listen for words or phrases that "pop" or stand out, whether it be a change in the voice, expression, or body language. Notice if emotions are expressed in words or the body. There might be a peculiar choice of word, or something to be curious about. Then ask the dreamer to repeat the dream—this could be either with or without her notes. There is no rush. Let the dream expand into the space between

you and the dreamer. In the second telling of the dream, begin to get clarification–the dreamer may mention a coat she put on–-I might have gotten
a picture in my head of a raincoat, but then she describes a tattered fur
coat that was her mom's. Big difference! Almost always there is a story
behind everything in the dream (an association) even when the Dreamer
doesn't make a connection at first, so stay curious. For now, though, we are
just collecting information and details, and then in the next chapter, we
will go into making associations with the images in the dream.

   Style of Listening. As a dream tender, know that everyone has their
own style when it comes to hearing a dream. Some people take no notes
and can hold the dream story in their head. Others jot down a few vital
words or notes. I am one who still writes down as much of the dream and
as many observations as I can. I might someday change that style, but for
now it helps me to relax. I also pay attention to what I sense in my own
body and thoughts that come up. I write them down and then let go of
them for the time being; later I might make an offering of these felt senses
and thoughts to the dreamer.

   Dream Told as Story. For the second telling of the dream, you might
have the dreamer tell the dream as a story. When the imagination is invited in, it can allow and encourage the dream images to develop. To the
dreamer, it might feel like she is making it up—that's okay. She can even
start with the phrase, "Once upon a time..."

Look and Listen in the Dream

You are observing the Dreamer with "soft eyes" that allow you to be present with the dreamer as she shares her dream, and simultaneously you
are listening for the following parts of the dream:

   Landscape. Where is the dream taking place and what is the time of
day? Describe in detail the setting. Notice colors and lighting. Is this scene
from the present or from the past?

   Characters. Who is visiting in the dream? Describe both people and
animals. Do you recognize them? How are they the same and how are
they different from awake life? Who is wanting your attention? Notice if
you are in the dream or watching it.

   Story. What are the highlights of the story? The end of the dream is
saying where the energy wants to go.

Dreamer's voice and body language. Pay attention to what words are said with a different resonance. Notice emotional reactions. What is the body saying, and what movements and gestures are made as the dream is shared?

Feelings. What feeling words are stated in the dream? What feelings are coming up in the dreamer? If a dream tender is present, notice what you are feeling as you observe and listen.

Peculiarities, word play, and opposites. What is the "unusual" in the dream? What is trying to get your attention? It might be a smell, or an object, or a person or animal that is out of context. What is repeated more than once? Contrast and similarities are also important to notice. Contrast might appear as water and land, night and day, open and closed. Similarities bring emphasis. Are there puns or double meanings of words? Here are some examples of puns and plays-on-words:

- **Pastel:** of the past
- **Reins:** reign
- **Mosaic:** broken pieces put back together
- **Altar:** alter
- **Stairs or elevators:** ascending or descending
- **Soles of one's feet:** soul
- **Cooking a steak:** Could there be something at stake?
- **Ice or food melting or defrosting:** What's thawing?

Questions for clarification and information:
- I'm curious about... Describe... Where... Say more...
- Who's visiting now?
- What's happening here?
- What gets your attention most in the dream?
- What are you most curious about in the dream?
- Where do you feel it in your body?
- I'm from another planet. Can you describe or explain to me what ___ is? (ie., What is a hose?)

What's Opening?

We have been gathering all the information and details of the dream by listening, watching, and asking questions. In this way, we activate the dream field and the body field by slowing down the process and being curious. Both of you, the dream tender and the dreamer, are in relationship as a space begins to open with landscape and characters becoming clearer and more visible. They receive your invitation to be seen and heard. Dream Psyche is very clever and might show up in one figure or image that could easily be overlooked, so be aware of what is hiding in the boring or dullness. For example, there might be a woman sitting over in the corner who says nothing, but she just watches. You might find as you begin to work with the dream that she is holding something in her lap, or she has something to say.

Dreamer and Dream Tender Trust the Process

Listen up! This is important. Keep in mind that the dreamer and the dream tender are not directly doing and leading this work if they are using the skills offered here. This new process of being open to who and what visits during the dream session as you invite in your guides and ask questions of curiosity, takes quite a bit of responsibility off the two of you. You are not alone in this process. Dreamer, if you are able to trust your inner guides, and the dream tender and group, then whatever comes up or doesn't show up is the way it is supposed to be. Dream tender, if you are giving room for visitations from guides and others along with listening to your intuition, then all is just what it should be. Yes, it will take practice. Yes, our egos have a lot to say, which we have to learn to keep in check. Be fascinated and gentle with yourselves and this process. Dream tender, explore and find your own style. Being good enough is good enough! Dreamer, if you hit a wall or don't want to share, later explore what happened. You are quite capable of continuing these unveilings on your own and with time.

Summary: Telling, Listening, and Exploring the Dream

1. **Four Gifts: Deep Listening, Not Knowing, Curiosity, and Patience.**
2. **If it's a nightmare:** go to Chapter 7 on Nightmares.
3. **Dream tending preparation:**
   a. **Relax:** by taking 3-5 deep breaths.
   b. **Connect:** with heaven and earth.
   c. **Call:** in your guides.

4. **Telling and listening to the dream present itself.**
   a. **Ask:** What dream is visiting?
   b. **Style of listening:** Some take few notes; some write complete dream.
   c. **Dream told as a Story:** Dreamer tells the dream like a story.
5. **Dream tender looks and listens for:**
   a. **Landscape:** Where is dream taking place? Details. What era?
   b. **Characters:** Who is visiting? Describe people and animals.
   c. **Story:** Tell the highlights of the story.
   d. **Dreamer's voice and body language:** Notice emotions, gestures, body.
   e. **Feelings:** What feeling words are from the dream? What feelings are present?
   f. **Peculiarities, word play, and opposites:** What is unusual in the dream?
6. **Questions for clarification and information:**
   a. **Ask:** I'm curious about... Describe... Where... Say more...
   b. **Ask:** Who's visiting now? What's happening here?
   c. **Descriptions:** I'm from another planet. Explain to me, for example, what a hose is.
   d. **Ask Dreamer: What are you most curious about?**
   e. **Ask Dreamer: Where do you feel it in your body?**
7. **What's opening?** Notice what is coming forward as dreamer answers questions.
8. **Dreamer and dream tender trust the process.**

Chapter 4:
ASSOCIATIONS &
AMPLIFICATIONS OF DREAM

So far, we have begun to develop the skills of deep listening and curiosity as the dreamer shares her dream. We are staying with these skills, plus the Not Knowing and patience as we continue to help the dream unfold. Dreamer or Dream Tender, you might have taken a few notes or noticed a few particular items that stood out more than other parts of the dream. It could be a word that is spoken with extra emphasis or said multiple times; it could be the unusual landscape or animals; it might be the dreamer's hand that keeps reaching upward as she speaks of the size of the flower. Dreamer, you might have explored books, references, and followed synchronicities that have come through as you explored the words and images in your dream.

This information often overlaps with this next step of guiding the dreamer into telling more of associations and connections that are coming up within this dream work. Maybe the dreamer had a woodcutter in the dream, and she is asked to describe the woodcutter. As she talks, she might start using the word woodman and you say, "woodcutter/ woodman." She says, "Oh, my gosh! I just purchased a book by Marion Woodman!" This leads to the exploration of what Marion Woodman holds for her. These associations and subsequent insights start opening the dream up.

Curiosity Questions

Dream tending is not a linear process, and so the previous chapter's questions and the story being told can easily overlap and flow into the dreamer making associations. Keep the sense of wonder and curiosity present. Remember to continue using the questions previously introduced; they help to release the veils that surround the dream picture:

- I'm curious about... Describe... Say more...
- Where do you feel it in your body?
- What comes up when you talk about your childhood dog?

If there is an animal in the dream, I have noticed that Dr. Aizenstat almost always follows and keeps the focus of his questions on the animal in the dream. Animal leads, we follow.

Associations

I woke up this morning with just a snippet of a dream and thought it was a dream with no substance. I doubted I would write it down because it seemed uninteresting. (Yes, I still have these thoughts!) But I have learned to write dreams down no matter what; I have almost ignored some of my most profound dreams because I thought they seemed meaningless or boring. The dream from this morning is short. *Corn wrapped in foil is cooking on the barbecue. I remove the burnt foil from the corn, and I am eating the most delicious and juicy corn ever! I am amazed.* Simple enough, ordinary enough and luckily enough, I wrote this dream down. I begin to imagine into the burnt outside of the foil, the yellow of the corn, the juicy sweetness as I start to bite into the corncob. Oh, my mouth actually starts to water! This image is still so alive in me. I have an inner and outer sense of the pleasant joy of a summer's day. To my surprise, as always, thoughts and memories begin to float in and visit. Corn. I'm from the Midwest so cornfields are everywhere. What do you do in Kansas? You "sit around and watch the corn grow" is an old saying to tease us Kansans. And then I remember the summers visiting my dad when he lived on Chesapeake Bay.

Driving down the road, we'd see a sign that said, "The Queen is In!" We would stop and get some Queen corn and cook it immediately after arriving home—delicious! Hmmm... The Queen is In. Something quivers within as I now hear that phrase. I explore what comes up around hearing it with different ears. The sense of a visitation fills me. This corn is definitely yellow corn, and this color seems quite vibrant and striking. I know

I will revisit this. I'm curious about what the color yellow means for me but also in the dream dictionary. Oh my! My thoughts jump to, "How I do miss my dad." We had such a sweet, delicious relationship. There was a slower pace and rhythm on those hot summer days. And as always with dreams, I continue to be surprised with what seems like a snippet of a dream—not worthy of unwrapping. I thought I was going to just enjoy the dream; sit with the dream. What richness I might have lost.

Associations with your Recent Events and Personal History. Following are some guidelines and questions that will help you open up associations in the dream. There will be the personal associations made to the dream such as, "We just fixed corn on the barbecue last night." Notice that I did not necessarily follow the steps in order. It is the Image that leads, and we follow. This is true for the unfolding also. After you've made all the personal associations, then begin to see what comes up next. The association of being at my Dad's in the summer begins to deepen into amplification as I share that I see the sign announcing, "The Queen is in," and also as I begin to reflect on the history of corn (maize).

Think about the events that occurred within the 48 hours preceding the dream. Dream tending shows us that there are many facets and layers, beginning with dream images and story, often being associated to recently experienced life events. It is important to explore this first to acknowledge and honor what is occurring in your day-to-day life. It could be emotional information of a grandmother passing away, or a simple connection, for example, we just cooked corn on the cob last night.

In addition to the last 48 hours, notice details that may situate the dream in your personal history. Be curious about what era of life. What is the age of the dreamer, how old are those figures in the dreams, and is the dream action taking place in the childhood home or where? Look for parallels between the issues in the dreamer's life then and her life now. Dreams have many layers, and there is generally this personal layer to explore before moving to the next, multiple layers.

Associations with Figures, Landscape, and Themes. Explore the figures, landscape, and themes by reflecting on each one about what comes to mind. For example, with barbecuing and eating corn, there is an association with summertime and cooking outdoors. Or we might be curious about aluminum foil, the meanings of foil, or the color black. In another dream situation there might be a visitation of a childhood friend that triggers the memory of the parents forbidding you from playing with him. What pain might be buried? If you are working with a dream tender, she should explore this material using love and respect, along with the tools of questioning.

Universal Themes of Dream Images

It helps to have a few ideas of what symbols can represent when beginning dream work. They give us hints and ideas of what to explore, especially when working our own dream as a beginner. Later, these might or might not be used; stay flexible in exploring what your dream image carries and not just assume these universal meanings are true for you. Trust your own gut feelings and intuitions as the final word. With that in mind, here are some basic general themes and meanings of images that might be useful as you enter into dream work.

- **Vehicles, houses, plants** can be symbolic of the Self and can be diagnostic for health.
- **Front of the house** represents what's in front of you or the back of the house, which could mean what's behind you, in your past, or something you are not seeing.
- **Colors** carry a frequency; red can be hot rage. But make sure you allow the dream and color to speak for themselves. Red might have been the color of your first car or the color of your mother's hair. So, don't box it into a category if the shoe doesn't fit. Also, explore the colors of the Chakras.
- **Water** can be a symbol for emotions or the unconscious.
- **Finding money** may be associated with discovering new riches, treasures, or finding that which is of value.
- **Baby or pregnancy** may be a new beginning or something that is being created or birthed.
- **Flying or rising above** can represent freedom or a denial of reality.
- **Numbers** can be very significant, so look them up in a reference book.
- **Shapes** can have meaning–the shape of a chalice might depict the feminine.
- **Nudity** may be associated with honesty, openness, or vulnerability.

when the alchemy of cooking has blackened the outer to prepare the inner bounty. How delicious is that!

Pause, Listen, and Reflect

Step back from the imagery and pause and wait every so often. Allow time for spontaneous associations and connections to occur betwixt and between the various levels of the dream space that you are sitting within. Listen in to what more wants to enter. If you have stayed with holding the images, story, and new material discovered, there can be this quiet tension that goes with waiting. Practice getting comfortable with this space—this "waiting room." Know that the *Other* is working behind the scenes—we just need to be available to receive. Be open to the unexpected. In the blink-of-an eye an insight might visit. After holding the pause, share what thoughts or feelings show up and then continue to use the questions to encourage thoughts, insights, and reflections to come forth.

Sometimes, carrying the dream with you throughout your day, reflecting on it, looking for aspects of it in your outer world can be helpful. I encourage you to wait within these pauses, and trust that these moments are just like a surfer waiting in the water for the next wave to come. This can happen in one sitting or one day or even weeks, as the insights roll in.

If there is a dream tender, it's helpful to say back to the dreamer what she has shared. It gives her a chance to clarify and to hear what she, the dreamer, has spoken. It also gives you, the dreamer, a chance to hear your self—it's amazing how powerful this can be. After this process, return to the dream and see what is noticed now. What is being revealed?

Coming Up for Air

Whether you are working alone or with a dream tender, you might either feel stuck, stopped, or at a standstill. Have you gone far enough or is this a pause? Some dreamers are new to the depth of this work and need or want to stop. Sometimes a gentle, respectful nudge is all that is needed to continue; it's as if you are swimming in the deep waters and need to come up for air, then a pause before diving back down. This could just be a quiet pause, but surprisingly, this place of coming up for air can also be accomplished by allowing a bit of humor to enter. There's nothing like a chuckle or laughter to help us pause and briefly step back, but this can't be forced—it must be natural and respectful in its timing and words. Many times, this humor allows for the dreamer to dive more deeply into the process.

Stop or Carry On?

With dream tenders and groups, the dreamer might feel like they have taken too much time—for people who do not always share their personal life, they could be feeling vulnerable, and this needs to be respected. Good feedback to such a dreamer would be to support them in their courage, and to share something you were personally touched by in their dream processing. In my experience, sometimes it is even more about the dream tender having the courage to make the leap into the next step of animating the images by asking the questions that open up this next field of animation and interaction as described in the next chapter. But if the dreamer is feeling complete, go to Chapter 6 where Closure of the dream work is addressed.

Summary: Association and Amplification of Dreams

1. Stay relaxed and in the Not Knowing.
2. Reflect a moment on your notes, if any, then let go.
3. Listen for guidance from intuition and guides (God, ancestors.)
4. Continue using curiosity questions:
    a. I'm curious about... Describe... Say more...
    b. Where do you feel it in your body?
    c. What comes up when you talk about your childhood dog?
    d. 'If an animal is present in the dream, follow the animal," says Aizenstat.
5. Associations with recent events and personal history:
    a. What has happened in last 48 hours?
    b. How old are you in dream or what time of life is it? What era is the dream?
    c. What's your relationship with those in your dream?
    d. Are there parallels between your life issues then and now?
6. Associations with figures, landscape, and themes.
7. Universal themes of dream images: for example, cars, house, plants symbolic of Self.
8. Amplification:

    a. Deepen the dream process with movement, art, voice, and/or poetry.

    b. Fairytales or myths that might connect with the dream.

9. **Pause, listen, and reflect:**

    a. Questions will have led to much sharing by dreamer.

    b. Dream tender reflects back to dreamer what she has said.

10. **Coming Up for Air:** Use humor, respectfully, to help dreamer come up for air (pause).

11. **Optional stopping place:** If you are ready to practice animating the images, continue to the next chapter. If dreamer is ready to stop, go to Chapter 6 and read about Closure.

Chapter 5:
ANIMATING AND INTERACTING WITH DREAM IMAGES

In a recent dream of mine, Hummingbird is holding Bat up to the light of a fixture. As I share this dream with my dream tending friends, I am intrigued that this part of the dream brings tears. I explore the image. I make my associations. It does not escape me that bats are creatures of the night. I explore the tears and the tenderness I feel for this beautiful little hummingbird working so incredibly hard to hold Bat up to the light. As I imagine into the hummingbird sitting in my hand, I look closely at its beautiful, iridescent colors. I feel his fine vibration and the trust he offers me. I stay completely quiet and watch as Hummingbird begins to poke at Bat and then buzzes back and pokes at my hand. What I realize about myself is that I am holding back from Bat. And so, as I hold out my left hand, my dream tender asks, "What opens up in Bat when you offer your hand?" Bat says he leads a lonely life; no one has ever offered a helping hand and he feels seen and acknowledged now. I am then asked, "What opens up in me?" Oh my! I feel this abundance of love for this creature of the dark.

Opening to Embodied Images

So far, we have learned to not rush the dream process. We have been learning to match the dream's rhythm and to listen to hear stories behind the dream story with the ears of our heart. The dream has brought forth and activated memories, thoughts, and feelings, along with fresh meanings appearing. As we enter its world as a guest, the dream and the images within the dream are beginning to wake up and are becoming more embodied and real. With imaginably animating the dream figures, you will be utilizing a way of seeing that originates from the inside out. This kind of looking requires a bit of magic—the kind of magic that we all are familiar with, or at least were at one time. Really, it is rather simple. You are recovering a way of seeing that you used often as a child, and still sometimes visits in rare moments as an adult. The secret is to see without focused intention. Using soft eyes or closed eyes and sensing the presence of the image in the room, allow your imagination to continue the dream story, as I did with the hummingbird.

Interacting with Dream Images

As we step into the field of animation, we begin to see that the embodied images have presence and pulse. Interacting with dream images deepens your relationship with them and allows you to get to know them more intimately. In so doing, we can begin to be in conversation with them. I continue to be in relationship with Hummingbird and Bat. As I sit and watch the hummingbirds buzz my flowers, I resonate more than ever with dream  Hummingbird. This type of dream work has brought incredible richness to my life as the outer and inner worlds are more connected and feed each other. With animating these dream figures by honoring them with our attention and believing in their realness, we can begin to dream the dream forward. In so doing, we invite the image to come to life; to become a living participant in the room with us.

Useful Questions

- Remember to use some of the curiosity questions from previous chapters, such as describe, say more, I'm curious about, notice...
- Who or what gets your attention most in the dream?
- Is there a particular image that has something to tell you?

- Do you see the presence of Bat? Where do you see him in the room? Do this with your eyes closed if you're comfortable doing so.
- When an image makes an appearance, dream tender could ask, what opens up...? And then explore thoughts and feelings. This begins a dialogue with the images and the dreamer. For example, what opens up in you when Tom the gardener hands you a flower? Dreamer might respond by saying: Softness, a sense of beauty. The dream tender then explores with the dreamer what that softness feels like or where it is in the body. The sense of beauty might want to be explored with a prompt: Say more. Listen to and follow the lead of the dreamer and images, possibly asking the question: What opens up in Tom the gardener when he hears this?
- Do you see how there is a back and forthness to this process as the dream is imagined into and then interaction occurs with images and dreamer dialoging. Notice that a relationship is developing. There is a presence of love in the room encompassing this exchange.
- Where do you feel it in your body? If this did not come up before, the dream tender asks the dreamer this question and then has her describe it.

Returning to the Dream

If you are working the dream by yourself, write down what has been revealed to you in your dialogue with the images. Write what feelings are present, especially if something has shifted within. Now read the dream with fresh perception.

If you have been working the dream with another person or group, the dream tender and the group have been a container helping to hold the dreamer's process. The dream tender facilitates a back and forth process between dreamer and images or one image to another. The dreamer is the one who decides when she is complete with her dream work and usually will open her eyes. Allow time for her to incorporate all that has been revealed by the Images. Usually there is an observable change in attitude and even physical appearance of the dreamer. Reflect this back to the dreamer for her to notice and absorb the shift you have witnessed. The dreamer might have new awareness that she may share—she and the dream tender will converse from this new place. Yes, the puzzle picture is becoming clearer, and the dreamer is getting clues about what she is hearing and feeling. Trust that "felt" sense and the relationship that is beginning to grow and is connecting all the different parts. The dreamer will know when this process is complete for now. The next chapter will help in bringing this dream work to closure.

Summary: Animating and Interacting with Dream Images

1. **Animation of dream images:** Questions dream tender might ask:
    a. Is there a particular part of the dream that wants or has your attention?
    b. Is there a particular image that has something to tell you?
2. **Open to embodied images** by imagining the presence of the image.
3. **Developing a close relationship with the image** as you imagine into it:
    a. Invite dreamer to use soft or closed eyes.
    b. Remember the way of Being you knew as a child. Invite in magic.
4. **Questions that help evoke images into interacting** with dreamer:
    a. Describe... Say more... I'm curious about... Notice...
    b. Do you see the presence of Bat?
    c. Do you see him in the room?
    d. When image makes an appearance, ask what opens up in you when Tom the gardener hands you a flower? or When you blush and say, thank you?
    e. Where do you feel it in your body?
5. **When image makes an appearance** explore the back and forthness; the reciprocity and dialogue.
6. **Returning to the dream from this place,** this place within that holds something new that wasn't there before and see what comes up.
7. **Does the original dream, the unknown puzzle, reflect back:** a picture, image, thoughts, and feelings that weren't there before or is there more clarity to them?
8. **Find where the dream wants to sit within you.** Feel a sense of completeness.
9. **Go to Chapter 6: Bring Closure to Dream Work.**

Chapter 6:
BRINGING CLOSURE TO
DREAM WORK

You have been exploring the different parts of the puzzle pieces of the dream, seeing some of the pieces fall into place as you, the dreamer, make associations. Along the way, there have been stories, memories and reflections that have been uncovered and shared. Aha's might be present for the dreamer as these discoveries are made. There will usually be a richness and some understanding that has entered with threads of information connecting and interweaving to begin revealing the Picture. The dream has revealed an aspect of something that it is wanting you to see and is showing you areas for curiosity and exploration. You will probably have the feeling of more is to be revealed over time, or so I hope. We never finish knowing all the layers and passageways within a dream. That is why this dream work is so alluring and intriguing!

Don't Get Discouraged

Don't give up if you feel you did not experience the dream unfolding or opening up as you had hoped. In my experience though, I have never seen a dreamer leave this process empty-handed, especially if the dream was tended with another person or group. Allowing the dream to just Be, to just exist inside and outside of you, is a wonderful honoring of the dream. If this is where you have stopped, remember to reflect and touch into the dream every day or so. Also, be looking in the outer world for the images to appear or trigger more reflections on the dream. This points us in the direction of doing less analyzing of a dream and instead continuing to explore the inner and outer worlds with the dream in mind. BE the dream work you have opened. Go experience the world through the eyes of the dream images.

Offerings from the Others

If you worked the dream with a partner or in a group, the dream tender might ask the dreamer if she wants to hear what other people have to "offer" as their personal insights or thoughts. It must always be clear in a group and with the dream tender, that we never tell the dreamer what her dream means, but we can make offerings of possibilities, as if we are setting them on a table in front of the dreamer for consideration. Many times it is someone in the group who hears a pun or a double meaning of a word or a name; there might be an association to a different part of the dream that is made by one of the individuals; a fairy tale could have come to mind; or a friend has a historical piece from the dreamer's past or another dream that seems like it fits. As these offerings are made, it is mainly the dream tender who helps to monitor the input from the group and to step in if there is someone overstepping the boundaries. The dreamer listens for what inwardly resonates from the outer input. This part of the tending can be the most profound, where someone's offering is the key needed for the dream work to come together.

The dream tender should offer the dreamer the last say on the dream; she is the final authority on what the dream means to her. Are there any last thoughts? Remember—dream work is soul work, and things could be shifting and moving at a deep level so Dreamer, be gentle with yourself. Dream Tender, encourage the dreamer to carry the dream with her as she journeys through the following days. James Hillman says, "It is not what you say about a dream after a dream, but the experience of the dream after the dream." So pay attention to what shows up and occurs, for that is part of the dream work/soul work.

Upon completing the dream tending, the group should take at least a 5 to 10-minute break before shifting to the next dreamer.

Summary: Bringing Closure to Dream Work

- **Does the dream work have a sense of completion** for dreamer and dream tender?

- **Ask the dreamer if she wants to open her dream to the group.** Be clear that others won't tell dreamer what they think the dream means. They can make offerings of possibilities. Dream tender is the gate-keeper and can stop the sharing or may help reframe the statement.
- **Sharing by others in group**—insights they have such as a fairytale that sounds like the dream, puns on words, feelings that came up for them, and historical information.
- **Encourage dreamer to carry the dream with her** as she journeys through the next days. Remember—dreams can stay alive and with us for long periods of time, also.
- **Dream tender offers dreamer the last say** as the final authority on her dream.
- **Dream work is soul work**—this is deep work, where things could be shifting that might not be visible. Be gentle with yourself. Take at least a 5-minute break between dreams.

Chapter 7:
NIGHTMARES ARE A BIG DEAL

Many times, it is a bad dream or a nightmare, possibly a recurring one, that motivates a person to seek more help in understanding her dreams. These nightmares can be terrifying, and the body reacts strongly to the fear present in the dream. Some worry that they might be possessed by the figure or traumatized by it. As terrifying as this can be, working with a nightmare can lead to profound transformation. It truly helps to hold the idea that nightmares come in such drastic and sometimes awful forms to get our attention for wholeness.

In one nightmare that visited me,

> *I hear a noise outside the house. I go out and reach to open a gate with the latch way up high. I go through the gate and some menacing men pull up in a car. With a pounding heart, I go back through the gate but can't get it locked. With the men right behind me, I run back into the house and lock the door. I wonder if they can get in.*

One of the first and foremost questions we ask or wonder about when a nightmare visits is What or Who is trying to get our attention? Dream Psyche sends us all kinds of messages and dreams that we pay no attention to, but then the time comes in our lives when, faced with issues, we are frozen or stuck. This frozen or stuck state is most often wrapped with fear. In my dream, what might I be locking out or locking in? Locks definitely are a significant image here. And who is visiting that I am wanting to shut out? Is Dream Psyche fighting fear with fear? Possibly. One thing we do know is that it does have our attention. We might be too frightened to go to sleep, fearing the dream will visit again, or we might wake up shaking and sweating. We awaken, relieved that the dream wasn't real, and yet our body is still trembling from its realness.

I suggest you not work with nightmares by yourself. Find a dream tender to help in this process. If there is no one to help you, then in the beginning, proceed slowly and cautiously with some distance. In my dream, I begin by looking for an image, an ally in the dream that is either already there or who shows up as I search. This can be a guide and loving figure who facilitates the encounter with the frightening figure. This ally will assist in your meeting with this image and helps create a separation so you can process what is occurring. In my case, there was not an ally figure within the dream, but an imaginal lion showed up by my side; I grabbed his mane for courage. You will discover as you make this encounter, the monstrosity of a figure can many times transform into your greatest ally, but if we are still in our fear, it can also undermine or desert us. Proceed with caution, and always stop if the anxiety level is not tolerable. If this should occur, you can use the art or writings to help facilitate the visitation of this image, and at the same time to provide a separation.

What are some of the things that you can do to stay close to these frightening images? The desire is to be able to allow the Intolerable nightmare figure to become tolerable, and then to actually have this figure become one of our greatest allies. Hard to imagine, I know, and you can't make this happen. It happens when the dreamer trusts the process, the dream tender, the guides, and especially the dream ally. For me, as Lion and I opened the door and I spoke with the ringleader, he began to transform into a deliveryman with a music box in his hands. The following steps will be helpful in tending nightmares.

Working with Nightmares

Nightmares come in frightening forms to get our attention.

I.   **Preparation for sharing the dream:** Remember to do the relaxation and breathing practice, and then call in your guides. The dreamer begins by telling the dream in first person, present tense.

2. **Dream tender listens and watches as dream is told:** We are using the techniques we have learned in Chapter 3, with dream tender listening and watching for the following:

    a. **Landscape:** Where is the dream taking place and what is the time of day? Describe in detail the setting. Notice colors and lighting.

    b. **Characters:** Who is visiting in the dream? Describe both people and animals. Do you recognize them? How are they the same and how are they different from waking life? Who is wanting your attention? Are you in the dream or watching it?

    c. **Story:** What are the highlights of the story?

    d. **Dreamer's voice and body language:** Pay attention to which words are said with a different resonance. Notice emotional reactions. What is the body saying? What movements does the dreamer use as she shares the dream?

    e. **Feelings:** What feeling words are used in the dream? What feelings are coming up in the dreamer? What are you, the dream tender, feeling as you watch and listen?

3. **Ask questions to get clarification:**

    a. **Ask:** I'm curious about... Describe... Where... Say more...

    b. **Ask:** I'm from another planet. Can you describe or explain to me what ____ is?

4. **Establish a Safe Place and Stop Signal:** What might this be for you? Imagine yourself on a sandy beach or you might be in the mountains by a stream. Let your imagination choose this spot. And then come up with a gesture that you will use with your dream tender to signal your need to Stop. This helps to create a separation that makes things tolerable and empowers the dreamer. Practice this.

5. **Dream tender, be respectful of the impact of the questions and watch for:** Heighten awareness of dreamer's body, watch for cues of increased breathing pattern, shakiness, fear. Slow down or go to Safe Place if dreamer becomes too aroused.

6. **Explore the dream using tools learned for association:**

    a. Who's visiting now?

    b. What's happening here?

    c. What gets your attention most in the dream?

    d. What are you most curious about in the dream?

    e. Where do you feel it in your body?

7. **Begin by telling the terrifying image:** I know that you know that I know you're here. This is a beginning place of acknowledgment.

8. **Look for allies in the dream:** The dream tender will assist you in finding an ally or allies within the dream to be a support figure. Dream tender asks dreamer, "Looking in the dream, is there anyone that you know who can help you?" If the answer is yes, then help dreamer befriend this ally figure. If not, ask the dreamer to use her imagination to ask for an ally, then wait and see who or what shows up. It might even be a hawk or a tree who can intervene and act on her behalf.

9. **Ally engages with the figure:** Dreamer, allow your Ally to engage with the nightmare figure. Do not engage directly at this point. Dream tender will use the questions that help animate the images. Does Ally see the figure in the room? Do you hear what Ally is saying to the figure? What does Ally say or notice? Does Ally feel it is safe for Dreamer to dialogue directly with Intolerable Figure? When your Ally and you are ready, go to the next step.

10. **What are you discovering?** Now notice what you are discovering about the intolerable figure. Is there a way to begin a dialoguing with this figure? Become curious by asking questions and listening and watching for its response. You are beginning to develop a relationship with this image and striving to get out of its grip that has terrorized you. What is the true nature of this figure? If the dreamer is unable or not ready to directly animate the Intolerable Image, then see if they could draw this figure. Ask if dreamer is able to dialogue with the figure in the drawing.

11. **Begin dialoguing with Intolerable Figure and notice the gifts.** When the dreamer is ready, begin animation and dialogue with this figure. Bring your ally along as you experience this figure and begin to explore and follow what it wants to show and tell you. Ask if the dreamer sees the figure in the room. Dreamer might point her finger. When the image makes an appearance, dream tender might ask the dreamer what this opens up for her. If dreamer has been able to dialogue and connect with this image, is she able to see the gifts they hold?

12. **Acting out the dialogue and the story.** After dialoguing in the imagination with these real figures, stand up and begin to act out the night-

mare story through dramatization. In my dream from earlier, I reach up to lock the gate. As I repeat this, the gate comes down lower and lower to a normal height, and then I practice opening and closing the gate with the Intolerable Figure watching. This helps me to then walk towards the Figure.

13. **Stop and check in with how you are feeling.** If there is an uncomfortable feeling in the body, are you able to locate it? See if an image or sensation or color comes to mind. Describe it to your ally and continue the dialogue work to help this to transform and release. If the symptoms have not diminished, then either go to your safe place or stop the dream work and do some relaxation techniques.

14. **If the figure still remains terrifying.** You might ask Dream Psyche, "Please send me a dream that helps to deliver your message in a less terrifying manner. You now have my attention." Terrifying dreams, over time, can begin to diminish as we do our work with later dreams. Keep revisiting the dream to see if any of the parts or feelings have changed. My experience has been that they can and do, in ways I never could have imagined. If the fear of the figure in the dream has not diminished after doing these steps, I would recommend finding a therapist who does techniques such as EMDR (Eye Movement Desensitization and Reprocessing), Tapping, or active imagination. This could be short-term therapy. If you want long-term therapy, there are many qualified therapists that could help you, but of course I would lean toward a therapist who uses dreams as their main focus of guidance.

15. **True warning or an exaggerated point?** It is so difficult to know if this nightmare of a dream is delivering a true warning or whether it is an exaggeration that needs tending. Since we don't know, it is important to give both their due. I can't tell you how to do this—you will have to explore your own intuitive gifts. What I can say is that usually it is Dream Psyche trying to make an exaggerated point because there is something important for you to learn from this. But please, if you are feeling the urge to check out other possibilities, do that. For example, if it feels like there is a health issue at stake, then make an appointment with your doctor, along with exploring what an alternative message could be from this nightmare figure.

Nightmares/Night Terrors in Children

As parents, it tugs at our hearts to have our children faced with bad dreams. Just like so many things in life, as much as we would like to protect our children from bad experiences and not have them happen, they will and they do. The best thing we can do is help develop resilience and mastery in our children. Following are some suggestions for helping your child not to be immobilized and frozen by these frightening images, and instead be empowered by disempowering the frightening images.

Listening and being Creative. In particular with nightmares, being a good listener and asking questions of curiosity is a good start. Begin by holding the child, if she wants, as she tells the dream; this helps give the child a feeling of safety. He might want to repeat it over and over again. Gather details by asking what color the witch's face is. If he says "Green!" this might lead to a discussion about how the witch might have made her face green. "With green paint," a child might say. This could lead to doing some painting. As a parent, use the creativeness you knew as a child to work with your own child to safely encounter the terrifying figure.

Allow these Images out into the Open. You might tire of hearing the child talking about how scary these images are, but it is important to not get discouraged. It might be you who is feeling helpless to help your child—recognize this and work to let it go. These images have way less power in the light of day than at night, so allow them forward to be talked out, acted out, colored out. The repetition helps to disempower and eventually dissolve these figures. Listen into whether the images are shifting or changing as they talk about them; keep following the child's lead. Keep in mind that stress can be the stimulus for nightmares so not only talking through the feelings is helpful, but also making some necessary changes in the daytime activities could be important.

Tools of Empowerment Showing Up. How might we empower our child against these frightening images or fearful situations? Remember to help them look for an Ally in the dream. Or you might ask her how she could make the witch move back. If the child doesn't have ideas or answers, you can suggest using a magic wand or throwing water on the witch. My granddaughter claps her hands or moves her legs (almost like feet running) to chase the scary figure away. You both could empower a particular stuffed animal with the power of protection for when the child goes to bed. Reading *Where the Wild Things Are* by Maurice Sendak can be useful in helping a child navigate through emotions and imaginatively engage with the wildness of the dream images.

Nightmares or Night Terrors? Generally, night terrors occur in the first two hours of deep sleep. The child awakens in terror with screams, sweats, eyes glazed, body movement, or sometimes sleep walking. They usually don't remember any dreams, do not want to be held, and they will go back to bed when encouraged. Night terrors can have a genetic component. The screams can be very arousing and frightening to those who are awakened by them. If these terrors don't subside over time, I suggest you seek help for the child.

Nightmares, on the other hand, occur during REM sleep and the child generally wants to be held, remembers a scary dream or sensations, and is scared to go back to bed. Both night terrors and nightmares can be exacerbated by stress or irregular bedtime schedules. It's important to keep in mind that if you have reason to believe that the terrors or dreams are pointing to something happening with or to your child in their waking life, seek out a counselor or physician.

Chapter 8:
DEEPENING THE DREAM:
LOVING THE DREAM IMAGES

For those of you who have been doing dream work for some time and would like to delve more deeply into the process to see what might emerge, here are some creative avenues for doing this work. Be satisfied with wherever you might stop in the process.

Try to spend some time each day with your dreams, writings, and art, by reflecting in silence, and developing a relationship with this inner life that is showing up in the outer world as you write, paint, and move. Be patient. Find your own style with the images. For me, as I deepen this work, there's a part that doesn't have a clue of what is occuring—I am just following urges from within by taking one step at a time. I am allowing something else to lead.

My ego says this is all nonsense, and I carry on with consciously ignoring it. I might say, this all feels stupid. I know, Ego, this is boring and a waste of time to you, but I'm asking you to take a back seat because I plan to continue. This process of proceeding despite the judgments of Ego is monumental in loosening up the controls it has over us. To be with the creative process from this place can take practice for most of us, and it is well worth it. It is such an invitation for Dream Psyche and Art Psyche to show up. You might play with Ego's words such as: you are wasting your time. Say back: I am going to have fun this morning wasting my time! Speaking of time, we are the chasers-of-time these days, but don't let time trip you up. If I only have a little time that day I say, I have 15 minutes and let's just see what comes forward. It's amazing what can occur. We are not after masterpieces, which is so freeing; we are learning to dialogue with the unconscious through creativity and imagination.

Opening the Creative Matrix

I begin by meditating/reflecting on the dream I have previously worked, taking five to ten minutes to slow down my breathing and allow the dream to become three-dimensional–alive, real, and present again. If I have already painted an art piece or written a poem, I prop it up four or five feet from me. Using soft eyes and the attitude of Not Knowing, I look at the piece for a few minutes. I might have an urge of what I want to do next or I will meditate on feeling energy move from my head to my hands. I rub them together, and like tracking or following an animal, I let the hands lead and I follow. What I have found is I don't fret about these things. If I've given over the pen or the pastel crayon to the process of the unconscious, this writing and making art has a spontaneous flow. Make it up if you must! What you are doing might not feel connected at all to the dream or other work. Go with it. Know that you are in a creative matrix, and it doesn't have to make sense. Every attempt might not have a resonance, but if you stay with it, something will eventually happen, and you'll definitely know you are on the trail of a dream adventure.

Using our Senses to Interact with the Dream Images

Experiment with using your physical senses to experience the figures and settings of the dream more deeply and immediately. For example, an image of a zebra appears in your dream. Can you imagine touching the zebra? What does it feel like? Look closely. Are you able to see its striped markings? Look for details. Can you imagine smelling this dream animal? Listen closely. Are there sounds being made either by the creature or in the surrounding dream setting? Describe those sounds: are they musical or raucous, loud or soft? Listen again, are you experiencing Zebra as an embodied dream image in the room with you? Using movement, see if you can become this animal. A connecting part might be writing a poem to Zebra or telling an African story of Zebra in the Wild, which you make up of course! Remember, all of the figures in your dreams have life and are alive—the animals, the plants, even the buildings and the stones.

Give Artistic Expression to your Dream Images

For me, the expressive arts have become one of the most fulfilling and enriching elements of dream work, and I am not an artist nor am I artistic. Meditate or choose a significant figure or feeling from your dream. Write a poem or draw, paint, or sculpt the figure or feeling. Again, let go of the demand for this to be art. Explore what your art piece opens in you. During this process I will *act* as if I am a writer or artist, allowing for something outside of myself to visit. By now there is usually another previous Dream or Image that connects in or an incident from my past that speaks up and off we go.

Art and Poetic Writing. This process of writing in itself seems to help open up the dream, and I will sometimes get hits as I write. For example, I had the following dream:

> *I enter an office with wooden bookshelves full of books and items gathered throughout the world. There's a picture up high and I need a step stool to reach it. I know that if I step up to get the picture off of the shelf that He will enter.*

I did not realize the profoundness of that last sentence until I went to write the dream down, and "Step Up" came through loud and clear. In the dream I am anxious. I remember the color lavender and the fluid feel in the picture. I found a picture on the Internet and accidentally put the photo paper in upside down. When I printed it, it came through the printer with these wet inks sitting on top of the paper and the colors as I had dreamed them! Meister Eckhart said, "When the Soul wants to experience something, she throws out an image in front of her and then steps into it." I stepped up by making an appointment with Russ Lockhart, the man who showed up in my dream. I took the artwork to share with him. Stepping Up, for me, is about experiencing the dream after the dream. It is about finally reaching out to someone I have yearned to meet and to acknowledge all that his writings have meant to me. I also shared a poem with him that I wrote, inspired by the art. I know there is even more to explore about who else might be entering with the name of He in the dream.

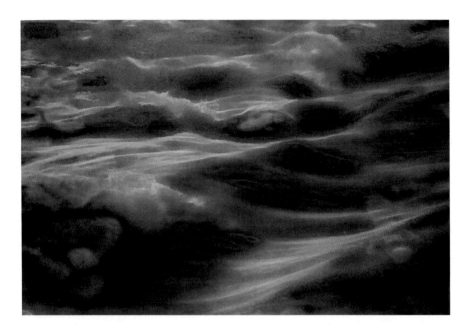

Stepping Up
He waits at the door wondering, watching
She so casually enters the room
Yet nervousness so present.
Eyes search and spot picture
Ahh, she is lured by the lavender ocean
that flows right through it.
Fluidity of color draws her in to reach high
And she knows
"If I step up, he will enter."
The foot stepped up
And in the "Blink of an Eye" nothing
Changed and everything changed
She was seen. She was witnessed
The threshold was crossed.

Linking Multiple Dreams. It seems every year or so I put together a journal or collage book of multiple dreams that are working me and are responding to each other. I don't always know this is clearly what is happening until I sit down and begin the process of putting together my story of the past six months or a year. I gather repetitive themes along with repetitive figures and landscapes. It's always a profound, unknowing experience that I mainly only have to give way to. Yes, it does take time, but it's not all at once. Usually a few dreams sit strongly within me and are hauntingly asking to be explored. There is always that sense of "Where do I begin?"

As I explained earlier, sometimes I begin with a simple, cryptic piece of drawing that I prop up, gaze at, and then I begin to write *whatever* comes up in me. It might feel related to the dream or not. This might lead to another piece of art that is different from the first piece. I can hear a voice chuckling in my head that says, "Really?" I've learned to forge ahead chuckling along with Chuckler. I might hear Aizenstat's voice saying, "Who's visiting now? Be curious..." or Lockhart's voice saying, "A dream loves a dream; art loves art." And I always add, and art loves a poem. I hold the feeling from the dream as I either respond with writing that is poem-like or with art. I have found these Images in my art carry great energy.

One example occurred in the Montana Dream Tending workshop, where Dr. Aizenstat tended my dream called "Rock Thrower, You Could Have Killed Me!" I had laid out my collage book open to the dream images from this dream. Great energies were stirred up as Rock Thrower definitely got my attention, and the dream guided me in what I needed to see. As I returned to my seat, the collage book remained open. The next dreamer started talking, and I couldn't focus. I realized my collage book was still open. I slipped over, closed it, and there was an actual sigh of relief in the room with several people thanking me. They were also having difficulty shifting, because the energy of Rock Thrower was still active in the room. Oh my! The power of this work!

A year after dreaming of Rock Thrower, where I am fearful and angry and frightened, Rock Thrower visited again in another dream. There is less fear and anger the second time around. The image depicts Rock Thrower casting his stone, and I duck or cower, but then I go down to the underworld where there is a merging of the figures. My dreaming, writing, and art continued, with the stone hitting me but not in a way I ever imagined. The day came when the merged fig-

ure from the underworld came up the stairs into the outer world, the stone sitting in the heart. These dreams continue to give, and I will continue to host them.

Collage Art. Another type of artwork is Collage Art (such as I used with my Rock Thrower dream). Whether you do it on a large sheet of paper or make a simple cardboard book with figures and landscape from the dreams, you simply go through magazines or old calendars, pulling out images and words

you are either drawn to or that represent the feelings, dream scene and characters from your dreams. They do not have to be exact. Cut or tear them, and then glue them down. Stay in a Not Knowing space as the picture unfolds; be ready for synchronicities and surprises. Check You-

Tube for ideas if you need more examples of the collage process, though there is definitely no right way to do this. Keep it simple, especially in the beginning.

Move and Dance with the Dream Images. Find suitable music and dance your dream. Become one of the figures—the animals, the people, and/or the objects. Move as they move or hold still as they do. This is an inner art; let go of wanting to be beautiful and graceful, or doing things right. Just move with the feelings of the figure and dance the mood of your dream. Let the rhythm generate from inside you or the image, and then allow the image to invite you to its dance. Having two or three people work together with movement is also very powerful. The dreamer does her movement piece to music, and the second person mirrors the movement back to her. If there is a third person, they play the role of being Witness to this dream dance.

Dream Becoming a Story. This can be a fascinating process as you allow the imagination to tell the dream story, and let it widen horizontally. If you take the fear or resistance out of the dream, how would the story carry forward? For example, I had a dream where a bulldozer was pushing a house towards mine, and I anxiously hollered, "Stop!" I took that dream and wrote this story forward without my character fearful of this house being pushed towards me. I could feel a shift within me that led me to not digging in my heels so much with some changes that were occurring in my life. Give your imagination permission to go in whatever direction it wants to as the story unfolds on the paper or at your computer. Have fun with this process and be ready for surprises.

Dreams are Meant to be Told

Other cultures, such as the Aborigine people, have known of the value of sharing dreams and have made it a part of their lives. In my life, my husband and I tell our dreams as we walk together in the morning. It works well for us because there is no rush and plenty of time for exploring and asking questions. It also helps us to share thoughts and feelings and history that is so easily bypassed in everyday conversations. With friends and family, dream sharing is a place of deep friendship where we meet in our telling. The conversation of the dream begins to bond us as we explore what the dream holds for the dreamer and the others. In this Deepening process, talking of the dream is usually a continual process over weeks and months. Your friend might have a dream that connects with your dream or she might be a support figure that helps to hold your dream, as you continue to explore. In the telling of the dream, all are impacted—the Dreamer, the Listener, the Images, along with the dream itself.

I try to make a point of contacting the people that are in my dreams to tell them the dream. I have to confess, though, that some people I have not contacted because I would be too embarrassed to share the dream! One particular person I contacted was a man I hadn't talked to for over ten years. In the dream he wasn't feeling well. In real life, I sent him a letter sharing the dream, and it turned out he had been dealing with terrible migraines. He called me immediately, and I encouraged him to go to the doctor—a brain aneurysm was discovered. He was grateful for the message, and I was grateful I delivered it.

What are You Discovering?

Know that there is no end game you are after. This is a process of exploring and honoring Dream Psyche and the unconscious so that you may develop a connection and pathway to your soul. Do not fret if you are feeling unsure and doubtful—if you can stay with that discomfort and keep breathing, it will shift. For those of you that are familiar with these processes and have tended your dreams, you will have more insights to weave into your dream work. These creative processes are helping everyone to physically develop different brain patterns, body patterns, and pathways. These processes lead to the imagination blossoming as old thought patterns and judgments are dismantled and new thoughts, images, and possibilities are being revealed.

Putting it All Together

Now I put my journal aside. I put on meditative music and set a timer, this can vary from 5 minutes to 30 minutes depending on the day and the depth of work I am doing. I am in a location where I know I will not be disturbed. I take deep, long breaths, and I have the practice of sending down a spiral root into the earth that anchors me. I travel back up this spiral and journey up through the body and connect with the heavens. From *this* place I have a meditative practice of a visualization developed from dreams that leads me to a place deep within. I recommend starting with visualizing a place that feels yummy and comfortable to go to, such as being on the beach with the ocean lapping the shore or near a creek on a sunny day. Chose a scene that fits for you. Picture yourself in this spot and enter the scene. Allow the scene to unfold and see who and what visits. I carry my morning's recorded dream with me in my memory as I enter this contemplative space. Sometimes the dream figures come to life and sometimes they don't.

This morning I had a dream where *I have a pie and as I dig into the edge of the pie with my finger, I find a melted Hershey's kiss of dark chocolate. There is this thick dark chocolate mixture that I bring to my mouth and my eyes even roll back with ecstasy because it is exquisitely delicious! A fellow named Brian, who I have never met in my day life, steps forward and I tell him to try the pie. He plops a smooth, dark chocolate bite in his mouth with the sound of hmm and then before I know it, he leans down and French kisses me as we both have this chocolate in our mouths. I then realize my daughter sees us. Oh, no! What will she think? End.* I wrote down after the dream: delight of seeing pie; curiosity of what it tastes like; delicious; must get Hershey kiss and eat it; Terrific kisser—wow! Passionate! Took me to my knees; melted me just like the chocolate; messy wonderful exchange; Shame of being seen; Thank goodness this happened in a dream and not real life; I want to enjoy that dreamtime kiss some more, because I can; I know I am not betraying my husband.

As I relax into this dream, I ask myself questions. Where am I? What does the pie look like in detail? As I imagine into my dream, I don't recognize the home I am in, but it is very cozy and comfortable. I am curious about Why now? It goes with what it is like to have pie—comfort and homey. From this meditative place, I allow myself to feel and sense back into the dream. I am not making associations or searching for meaning, I am just reliving this dream as I explore the sensations in my body. Of course, that kiss lures me right back in and makes my mouth water. I notice the startle of the spontaneous, unexpected gesture out of nowhere of the kiss and how immediately I surrendered to it. I check in my body where I feel the sensations. I know Shame has to be addressed, so I locate it both on the right side of my body and deep in my gut. The tears begin to flow because of how deeply I feel the Shame within.

A wise figure enters the scene, and I share the sense of shame with her. I can already feel it losing its grip on me, and I smile as I share the Chocolate French Kiss with her. Staying with Brian and the Kiss, he and I climb into a giant, gooey dark chocolate mud pie and roll around in laughter and passionate kisses. Such a joyful muddy mess as She looks on. For now, Shame has taken a step back; I know it is there, but I am able to stay with the joy and how it enlivens my body.

This meditative state and what it delivers always offers something different and new. There is no formula to be offered here—only the encouragement of staying open to visitations. I always hold the sense of inviting in that which is from the highest realm.

As I return from my meditation, I record my journey. Either now, later in the day, or the next day or so (we are all dealing with time), I begin the process of looking more closely at my dream. In some ways, the freshness of the dream makes it easier, but at times I have found that a little distance helps. The way a phrase is written, or a word is used will catch my attention in a way it didn't when it was so real in me. Either way or both ways, I begin the process of looking at the landscape of the dream, the Story and Characters of the dream, the feelings, the puns, which words carry more energy than others.

I tell the dream to my husband and later to my girlfriend as we walk. My girlfriend says, did it cross your mind that the name Hershey has both Her and She in it? My mouth drops open because of what she says but more so because of the resonate feeling inside that was triggered when she said it! Oh my...the chocolate kiss that he and I both enjoyed began to take on a sacredness of the She. The divine feminine that visited in my meditation is actually present in the "presence" of the chocolate kiss. And I also realize that He is within the word She. This totally begins to change the kiss, and Shame is dissolving in the presence of She. The tears of the knowing of what separates us help dissolve old fears and feelings so that my essence can join with Eros—with love. Do you see that this is not about falling in love with an outer man, especially since I truly love my husband. It is about falling in love with a more rounded, complete Self—He and She uniting within.

The ego comes into both dreamtime and daytime reminding us with a wagging finger, "This person is **not** your husband," short-circuiting something in the psyche thus denying Eros, that is trying to come into being. We get so literal and caught in the daytime rules, and can lose the symbolism the soul so sweetly provides like the chocolate kiss. James Hillman says it so beautifully, "...there is a loving in dream-work. We sense that dreams mean well for us, back us up and urge us on, understand us more deeply than we understand ourselves, expand our sensuousness and spirit, continually make up new things to give us—and this feeling of being loved by the images permeates...relationship." We have to be brave and allow ourselves to be loved by the images—*that* is what the dream is asking of us.

Chapter 9:
YOUR LIFE WILL NEVER BE THE SAME

Out beyond ideas of wrongdoing and right doing,
there is a field. I'll meet you there.
When the soul lies down in that grass,
the world is too full to talk about.
Ideas, language, even the phrase "each other"
doesn't make any sense.
The breeze at dawn has secrets to tell you.
Don't go back to sleep.
You must ask for what you really want.
Don't go back to sleep.
People are going back and forth across the doorsill
where the two worlds touch.
The door is round and open.
Don't go back to sleep.

–Rumi

How Might Your World be Different by Tending Dreams?

If you choose to explore your dreams and make them a part of your day-time world by giving life to dreams and images, you are not only doing your soul work, you are helping to create the future. By bringing in your guides, ancestors, and angels you are inviting in a world with a potential that might even be unimaginable for us. I believe these images, God or whatever you want to call these higher powers, need us as much as we need them. They need us to help hold open the portal entries with our desires and yearnings. We can't do it alone nor can they. Imagination is the key. Can it be that simple? Does it mean there will be no monsters or darkness? No, but it does mean we are given the tools with which to make our way through these difficulties and to actually find the light in the dark. So many famous people through the ages have discovered these mysteries and have made the teachings available to us if we are ready.

Our Inner Work Changes the Outer World

Especially in the beginning, as I was working with my dreams and spending time reflecting and doing creative projects, I wondered if I was wasting my time. Does this dream work and inner work really do anything or change anything? Years have now passed, and I now know, beyond a shadow of a doubt, that I have not wasted my time, and that, yes, this work brings change and transformation. I have personally experienced a tremendous change within myself of calmness, centeredness, joy, and love. I have seen firsthand the impact in my outer world, and what I now know, believe, and practice is that this inner work can change our outer world.

Carl Jung was fond of telling this story, told to him by his friend Richard Wilhelm, of a drought being broken in a village in China by a Taoist rainmaker:

> "There was a great drought where Richard Wilhelm lived; for months there had not been a drop of rain and the situation became catastrophic. The Catholics made processions, the Protestants made prayers, and the Chinese burned joss sticks and shot off guns to frighten away the demons of the drought, but with no result. Finally, the Chinese said, "We will fetch the rain maker." And from another province, a dried up old man appeared. The only thing he asked for was a quiet little house somewhere, and there he locked himself in for three days. On the fourth day, the clouds gathered and there was a great snowstorm at the time of the year when no snow was expected, an unusual amount, and the town was so full of rumors about the wonderful rainmaker that Wilhelm went

to ask the man how he did it. European fashion he said: "They call you the rainmaker; will you tell me how you made the snow? "And the rainmaker said: "I did not make the snow; I am not responsible." "But what have you done these three days?" "Oh, I can explain that. I come from another country where things are in order. Here they are out of order; they are not as they should be by the ordinance of heaven. Therefore, the whole country is not in Tao, and I also am not in the natural order of things because I am in a disordered country. So, I had to wait three days until I was back in Tao and then naturally the rain came."

C. G. Jung, Mysterium Conjunctionis

Some of the events in our world today are like the catastrophic drought in the rainmaker story, and we can get caught up in the political soap operas that hijack our energies and our emotional states along with our relationships with each other. I believe that we can be aware of the dramas, not ignore them, and truly believe that our inner work and inner world is "the way" toward change in the outer world.

Worlds Behind Worlds, Worlds Beneath Worlds

You will literally be changing the makeup of your brain and the senses in your body. You will be carrying with you the mystery that there are worlds behind worlds, under worlds, upper worlds, upside-down worlds, all available to us and impacting us whether we choose to pay attention or not. These worlds have figures that are accessible, and they want to help guide us. If we do choose to pay attention, we can witness and participate in these multiple dimensions. We can learn to allow dramas to unfold without being trapped in them because the story is much bigger than that. This was shown to me in my dream "Where's the Ammo?"

I am in a building and there are two teams. We are fighting each other with weapons. I'm left-handed and I'm having a difficult time shooting around right corners. Soon, I'm out of ammunition and I start shouting, "Where's the Ammo!?!" Somebody points to a door, and I open it to realize in the nick of time that it is enemy camp! Oh, no! I slam the door. A team member points up and says to go to the third floor. I run up the stairs, charging through the door shouting, "Where's the Ammo!?!" The people in the room are relaxed in chairs and one says, "It's much bigger than that." I again say, "No. You don't get it—where's the ammo!?!" And again, someone else says, "It's much bigger than that." They offer me a chair. I sit down and I start to relax; a calmness of the big picture comes over me. And then it is like a rocket ship and we lift off.

Luckily, I reflected on this dream a bit before heading to work, and it helped me with a situation full of tension and angst that I encountered at work. By remembering and reflecting on this dream, I was able to rise above it fairly quickly because the attitude shown to me in the dream gave me the conscious tools of dealing with adversity in the midst of a battle. This led to the situation resolving itself by early afternoon. I know I would have been caught in a combative situation for days if I had not reflected on the dream. This has been a dream that I've shared multiple times, and others have told me how it has shown up to remind them of taking the high road when they've been in a conflictual situation.

Engaging and experiencing life, nature, and dreams as alive brought a newfound depth of beauty and joy for me. It is as if I am seeing life through different lenses. When I wear these lenses, I can't help but feel the

glimmer of mystery. There is a felt sense of knowing there is something or someone much bigger than me at work behind the scenes. And this is what makes the art of dream tending unique and alluring. Once you step over the threshold into believing everything around you is real and has a life of its own, synchronicities begin to occur, new people come into your life, your body begins to resonate with an energy not previously known, and feelings open up. As you work with your dreams, they will become your friends, your guides, your mentors. Underneath this work is such a presence of love. And when you are able to come from this place of love, you cannot go wrong in working with dreams. Love has patience, tolerance, kindness, and respect. Love helps open the door to the mystery that waits on the other side of the threshold. Or as Rumi said, "Out beyond ideas of wrongdoing and right doing, there is a field. I'll meet you there."

Appendix A:

SUMMARY OF STEPS: WORKING WITH YOUR DREAM

Telling, Listening, And Exploring the Dream

1. **Four Gifts: Deep Listening, Not Knowing, Curiosity, and Patience.**
2. **If it's a nightmare:** go to Chapter 7 on Nightmares.
3. **Dream tending preparation:**
   a. **Relax:** Take 3-5 deep breaths.
   b. **Connect:** with heaven and earth.
   c. **Call:** in your guides.
4. **Telling and listening to the dream present itself:**
   a. **Ask:** What dream is visiting?
   b. **Style of listening:** Some take few notes; some write complete dream.
   c. **Dream told as a story:** Dreamer tells the dream like a story.
5. **Dream tender looks and listens for:**
   a. **Landscape:** Where is dream taking place? Details. What era?
   b. **Characters:** Who is visiting? Describe people and animals.
   c. **Story:** Tell the highlights of the story.
   d. **Dreamer's voice and body language:** Notice emotions, gestures, body.
   e. **Feelings:** What feeling words are from the dream? What feelings are present?
   f. **Peculiarities, word play, and opposites:** What is unusual in the dream?
6. **Questions to ask dreamer for clarification and information.**
   a. I'm curious about... Describe... Where... Say more...
   b. Who's visiting now? What's happening here?

    c. **Descriptions:** I'm from another planet. Explain to me, for example, what a hose is.

    d. What are you most curious about?

    e. Where do you feel it in your body?

7. **What's opening?** Notice what is coming forward as dreamer answers questions.

8. **Dreamer and dream tender trust the process.**

Associations & Amplifications of Dream

1. **Stay relaxed and in the Not Knowing.**

2. **Reflect a moment on your notes, if any, then let go.**

3. **Listen for guidance from intuition and guides (God, ancestors).**

4. **Continue using curiosity questions:**

    a. I'm curious about... Describe... Say more...

    b. Where do you feel it in your body?

    c. What comes up when you talk about your childhood dog?

    d. "If an animal is present in the dream, follow the animal," says Aizenstat.

5. **Associations with recent events and personal history:**

    a. What has happened in last 48 hours?

    b. How old are you in dream or what time of life is it? What era is the dream?

    c. What's your relationship with those in your dream?

    d. Are there parallels between your life issues then and now?

6. **Associations with figures, landscape, and themes.**

7. **Universal themes of dream images:** for example; cars, house, plants are symbolic of Self.

8. **Amplification:**

    a. Deepen the dream process with movement, art, voice, and/or poetry.

    b. Fairytales or myths that might connect with the dream.

9. **Pause, listen, and reflect:**

    a. Questions will have led to much sharing by dreamer.

    b. Dream tender reflects back to dreamer what she has said.

10. **Coming up for air:** Use humor, respectfully, to help dreamer come up for air (pause).

II. **Optional stopping place:** If you are ready to practice animating the images, continue to the next chapter. If dreamer is ready to stop, go to Chapter 6 and read Bringing Closure to Dreamwork.

Animating & Interacting with Dream Images

1. **Animation of dream images**—Questions dream tender might ask:
   a. Is there a particular part of the dream that wants or has your attention?
   b. Is there a particular image that has something to tell you?
2. **Open to embodied images** by imagining the presence of the image.
3. **Developing a close relationship with the image as you imagine into it:**
   a. Invite dreamer to use soft or closed eyes.
   b. Remember the way of Being you knew as a child. Invite in magic.
4. **Questions that help evoke images into interacting with dreamer:**
   a. Describe... Say more... I'm curious about... Notice...
   b. Do you see the presence of Bat? Do you see him in the room?
   c. When image makes an appearance, ask: What opens up in you when Tom the gardener hands you a flower? What opens up in Tom when you blush and say Thank you?
   d. Where do you feel it in your body?
5. **When image makes an appearance** explore the back and forthness; the reciprocity and dialogue.
6. **Returning to the dream from this place:** this place within that holds something new that wasn't there before and see what comes up.
7. **Does the original dream, the unknown puzzle, reflect back:** a picture, image, thoughts, and feelings that weren't there before or is there more clarity to them?
8. **Find where the dream wants to sit within you:** Feel a sense of completeness.
9. **Go to Chapter 6: Bringing Closure to Dream Work.**

Bringing Closure to Dream Work

1. **Does the dream work have a sense of completion** for dreamer/ dream tender?

2. **Ask the dreamer if she wants to open the dream to the group:** Others do not tell the dreamer what they think the dream means. They can make offerings. The dream tender is the gatekeeper.

3. **Sharing by others in the group:** Insights they have such as a fairytale that sounds like the dream, puns on words, their feelings, and historical information.

4. **Encourage the dreamer to carry the dream with them** as they journey through the next days.

5. **The dream tender offers the dreamer the last say on the dream.**

6. **Dream work is soul work:** this is deep work, where things could be shifting that might not be visible. Be gentle with yourself. Take at least a 5-minute break between dreams.

Appendix B:

SUMMARY OF STEPS: WORKING WITH NIGHTMARES

Nightmares come in frightening forms to get our attention.

1. **Preparation for sharing the dream:** relaxation and breathing techniques. Call in guides.

2. **Dream tender listens and watches as dream is told:** landscape, characters, story, body language, voice, and feelings.

3. **Ask questions to get clarification:** I'm curious about... Describe... Where... Say more...

4. **Dreamer connects with strength and establishes a Safe Place and a Stop signal.**

5. **Dream tender—be very aware and respectful of the impact of questions you ask the dreamer:** Awareness of dreamer's body; watch for cues of increased breathing, shakiness, fear. Slow down or go to Safe Place if dreamer seems to be too aroused.

6. **Explore dream tending using tools learned for association:** Who's visiting now? What's happening here? What gets your attention most in the dream? What are you most curious about in the dream? Where do you feel it in your body?

7. **Say indirectly to scary image:** I know that you know that I know you're here.

8. **Look for allies in dream.** Dream tender assists this process with dreamer.

9. **Ally engages figure.** Use questions we used when animating: Does Ally see him in the room? Do you hear what Ally is saying to the figure? What does Ally say or notice? Does Ally feel it is safe for dreamer to dialogue directly with image?

10. **What are you discovering?** Dream tender and dreamer explore before continuing. Ask if dreamer is able to dialogue with this figure. If dreamer is unable to begin a dialogue with this figure, she can draw the figure.

11. **Begin dialogue with Intolerable Figure and notice gifts.** When dreamer is ready, begin animation/dialogue with figure. Do you see him in the room? Where? When image appears, you might ask what opens up in you?

12. **Acting out the dialogue and story.** Act out or move with the dialogue or a part of the story, repeating it until fear diminishes.

13. **Stop and check in with dreamer**, asking how are you feeling?

14. **If figure remains terrifying**, ask Dream Psyche for a dream that is less terrifying. Encourage seeking the help of a therapist if nightmare continues to haunt dreamer.

15. **True warning of nightmare or an exaggerated point?** Explore both.

Appendix C:

Recommended Books to Read

- *Dream Tending* by Stephen Aizenstat
- *A Little Course in Dreams* by Robert Bosnak
- *Psyche Speaks* by Russ Lockhart
- *Dancing in the Flames* by Marion Woodman and Elinor Dickson
- *The Natural Artistry of Dreams* by Jill Mellick
- *Coming Home to Myself* by Marion Woodman and Jill Mellick
- *Dream Time with Children* by Brenda Mallon
- *Beginner's Guide to Jungian Psychology* by Robin Robertson (if you would like to begin to explore Carl Jung and his ideas.)
- *Blue Fire* by James Hillman
- *Drawing on the Dream: Finding My Way by Art* by Denise Kester
- *Women Who Run with the Wolves* by Clarissa Pinkola Estes
- *The Book of Symbols: Reflections on Archetypal Images* by Taschen
- *The Little Giant Encyclopedia of Dream Symbols* by Klaus Vollmar
- *Animal-Speak Pocket Guide* by Ted Andrew

Illustrations

Cover:

- The Sorceress is a painting by John William Waterhouse, completed between 1911 and 1915. It is his third depiction, after Circe Offering the Cup to Ulysses and Circe Invidiosa, of the Greek mythological character, Circe.

Chapter 1: Why I Tend My Dreams

- Japanese Lanterns, Luther Emerson van Gorder, 1895
- Soaring Violin, Marilyn's Collage Book
- Dead End Job, This Way Out- Sign Logo Art Way Out Grunge, ID 12466555 Kevynbj/ Dreamstime.com

Chapter 2: Remembering and Tending Your Dreams

- Vasilisa, An illustration for the Russian fairy tale, 1899 "Vasilisa the Beautiful" by Ivan Bilibin

Chapter 3: Telling, Listening, and Exploring the Dream

- On the Other Side of the Veil, by Michael Hague; The Enchanted World, Seekers & Saviors, Time Life Books. Page 72
- Angel Photograph by Marilyn, Notre-Dame de Fourviere, La Grace d'une Basilic que Lyon, France

Chapter 4: Associations & Amplifications of Dream

- Follow the Animals, by Michael Hague; The Enchanted World, Seekers & Saviors, Time Life Books. Page 71
- A Mermaid by John Williams Waterhouse, Enchanted World, Water Spirits. Time Life Books
- Miss Ellen Terry as Lady Macbeth, John Singer Sargent, 1912

Chapter 5: Animating and Interacting with Dream Images

- Fisherman Urashima, by Michael Hague; The Enchanted World, Water Spirits,Time Life Books pg. 108

- Hummingbird, Green violet ear sitting on Branch, ID 143922451, Jiri Hrebicek/Dreamstime.com

Chapter 6: Bringing Closure to Dream Work

- She Finds the Key, Denise Kester, Drawing on the Dream. She looked for the key for a long time and found it, only when she realized she was the key.

Chapter 7: Nightmares are a Big Deal

- Feeding the Intolerable, Willi Glasauer, The Enchanted World, Fabled Lands, Time Life Books, page 79

Chapter 8: Deepening the Dream: Loving the Dream Images

- Lamia and the Soldier, John William Waterhouse; The Enchanted World, Fairies & Elves, Time Life Books, page 117
- Lavender Ocean, Marilyn
- Rock Thrower, Collage Book, Marilyn
- Rock Thrower Visits Again, Art Book, Marilyn
- Grouping of Art Collages, Marilyn and World Dream group 2018

Chapter 9: Your Life Will Never be the Same

- Open Gate in the Countryside, ID 174769597, Garryuk/Dreamstime.com
- Heron in Flight, ID 168840733, Mwphoto55/Dreamstime.com

About the Author

M arilyn O'Brien attended Pacifica Graduate Institute (PGI) and received her master's degree in Counseling Psychology with a specialization in Depth Psychology. During her time at Pacifica Graduate Institute getting this degree, she discovered her love for dream tending. This led to her developing River Dream Workshops, where she guided women on river rafting trips followed by a weekend of dream tending. The combination of such an exhilarating experience of nature at her best, combined with soul at her best, made for a powerful, river dreamwork experience. Marilyn continued to develop her career and became a licensed clinical psychologist. Through the years, she continued her work and studies, which led her back to PGI to continue more in-depth programs of working with dreams.

Marilyn continues her rich life with her husband, living in Northern California on the Sacramento River. She is the grandmother of 8+ grandkids. Her grandkids inspire her to be playful and imaginative as she hosts butterfly tea parties or magical nighttime parties with the little munchkins taking lanterns out into the yard and playfully giving gifts back to nature. This same form of playfulness/soulfulness is part of a yearly event she hosts called World Dream. Women come from all over Northern California offering dreams that are not just their personal dreams but are also dreams for the world and from the world. What Dream loves most in these gatherings is the community that is formed by the sharing, eating together, laughter and tears. Marilyn continues to share her love of dream with others through her presentations, workshops, dream groups, friendships, and now through her book.

Made in the USA
Las Vegas, NV
05 July 2021